OUTSHINE

OUTSHINE

8 STEPS TO START MAKING IT HAPPEN

Shemin Nurmohamed

A Carbon Leadership Initiative

First published in 2017 by FAQS Books

ISBN 978-1-911195-61-0

Also available as an ebook
ISBN 978-1-911195-60-3

Typeset by Jill Sawyer Phypers
Cover design by Emma J. Hardy

Printed in Great Britain by Clays Ltd, St Ives plc

CONTENTS

To Aliya, Qaahir and Fayyaz – the shining lights of my life

INTRODUCTION

'In the future, there will be no female leaders.
There will just be leaders.'
Sheryl Sandberg, Facebook COO

I'M WRITING THIS FROM a hotel room at a technology industry trade show. There are 6,000 delegates here. Only 100 of them are women. That's little more than a paltry 1%. It leads me to wonder (not for the first time in this type of situation) about the many reasons why women have made the choice to opt out of the senior roles that would have secured them a place at the conference. I ask myself why is it, four years after 'Lean In' that little seems to have changed? Why is it that men still outshine women, with the lion's share of the limelight and the recognition that comes with it?

I'm an anomaly here, and whilst I feel welcome, it's no wonder that many women who attend such events doubt their deservedness and qualification, or are plagued by the nagging suspicion that they've been invited to fill a quota.

Although 20 years ago at an equivalent conference I may have been the only woman, the sclerotic rate of progress is an indictment of a system that's broken. Rather than making me angry, this makes me feel sad. Tech is a great industry to work in; it's surprisingly flexible, innovative and dynamic and the women who work in the sector are overwhelmingly supportive of one another. Many women are missing out on this.

HARD FACTS

I believe that building supportive communities of women (and men), are at the heart of any solution to the 'reverse pyramid' problem in the workplace. We need to form these communities to create a nurturing base from which the next generation of female leaders can draw the strength they need to outshine the competition. At entry level, women make up 46% of the corporate workforce. But the proportion dwindles swiftly as we move up through the hierarchy. A 2016 report based on research from a study jointly conducted by McKinsey and Leanin.org tells us that women make up 37% of managers, 33% of directors, but only 29% of senior VPs and 19% of C-suite (top senior executives) in the US.[1] Similar figures show that women hold 17% of executive committee roles in Europe.[2] Just 7% of FTSE 100 companies are led by a female CEO, whilst in the US in 2017, even fewer – 5% of Fortune 500 companies have a female CEO.

---

1. www.womenintheworkplace.com/

2. www.mckinsey.de/files/161206_women_ matter_2016.pdf

Research by Hewlett Packard showed that when identically well-qualified men and women were presented with an opportunity for promotion, men believed they could step up to the challenge if they met 60% of the criteria, whereas women only felt capable if they met 100% of the job requirements.[3] As a result, they didn't feel well qualified enough to apply for the position – in other words, they felt that the choice wasn't there for them to take. They believed that the requirements were a necessity – a prerequisite for being considered, so they ruled themselves out for not meeting all of them.

Likewise, a US study by Jennifer Lawless, Assistant Professor of Political Science and Public Policy at Brown University, confirmed the same phenomenon at work in politics. When researchers canvased 3,800 eligible candidates (women and men working at the highest levels in a range of professions), men were significantly more likely to consider themselves qualified to run.[4] The fact that running for office is a viable option, it seems, just didn't occur to the majority of the women questioned. Many of them simply assumed that the choice wasn't theirs to make. Their sense of the possible, in terms of their career, was profoundly restricted by their own limited thinking. They were knocking themselves out of the running before the starter pistol had gone off.

---

3. www.hbr.org/2014/08/why-women-dont-apply-for-jobs-unless-theyre-100-qualified

4. Citizen Political Ambition Study (Brookings, 2001).

In some instances, women are put off particular careers (politics) or sectors (tech, engineering and finance), because they have a gendered image. Tech is overwhelmingly male, one of a range of industries suffering from a dearth of female talent, particularly at the uppermost reaches of organizations.

It's interesting that the majority of women in tech work in the more traditionally 'female' areas – marketing and support. However, the small number of women who have carved out careers in other areas of the industry – the site managers and salespeople who I meet at the conference – share their overwhelmingly positive experience of the benefits of their less conventionally 'female' roles.

It's my belief that there's a huge perception gap. Many people have an outdated view of what commercial, client-facing jobs and senior roles in general entail and assume they are inflexible. I know this prejudice exists because I was guilty of it myself. I started out in finance, working my way up to CFO roles before I had my first child. I was able to work from home and dictate my hours, but was surprised to find when I moved into sales that I had more autonomy and flexibility than before. I had thought the opposite would be true.

Once I realized this, I became evangelical about spreading the word so that other women might consider a wider range of roles, whatever their life-stage. With the onset of more automation, the physical demands are evolving and opening up. And this trend will only continue. The work environment is expanding and there are more opportunities than ever for women to advance.

THE POWER OF UNCONSCIOUS CHOICES

It's sometimes hard to convince people of this, however. At IBM I was actively hiring women, not on a quota basis, but I was doing everything I could to encourage women to apply for the jobs that came up in my department. Despite this, for one senior job, of the 50 or so applicants we had, only three were women. One of them dropped out before the interview process began.

This 'not for me', mindset kicks in early on in women's careers. In her brilliant book, *Lean In*, Sheryl Sandberg gives an example of young women limiting their sense of choice prematurely. She talks of female executives having their perspective distorted, with one eye on an imaginary future, planning for a 'parenting friendly' (and thus circumscribed) career path, in some cases years before they have even found a partner. She quotes the author Alice Walker, who says that 'The most common way people give up their power is by thinking they don't have any.'

Hearing this, many of us will nod. But it's tougher to acknowledge the fact that perhaps it applies to *you*. You who may think of yourself as a feminist, with a successful career, healthy self-esteem and a life plan. Despite all this, it's still likely that, simply because you're a woman, you have made some unconscious choices along the way that are self-limiting.

The incremental impact of millions of women making these unconscious choices is that the pipeline of candidates for certain industries simply isn't there. When I'm recruiting, I often find myself asking where all the women have gone.

Over several years, I've devoted myself to understanding this problem in depth. I've also committed to learning everything I can about what helps women fulfil their potential, and I've thought a lot about how to modify the culture of the businesses I've worked in to enable them to attract more female applicants.

BUILDING A NETWORK

My quest turned me into a magpie for advice cherry-picked from a range of sources. I immersed myself in countless self-help books on every aspect of work. I studied what psychologists and social scientists have to say about gender in the workplace, and thought a lot about management style, culture and time management. Although all this advice was valuable, I found that it lacked the first step. Before getting started on a process of change, it's essential first to create the right mental environment to underpin lasting change in our lives. We must demonstrate leadership over ourselves.

It was with this in mind that, along with two colleagues, Marine Aubin and Georgina Hill, I began to develop Carbon Leadership. Carbon is a supportive network of likeminded women interested in helping to shape and support female leaders of all ages and at all stages of their careers – aspirant leaders included! Through our events, mentoring programmes and with this book, we aim to inspire women to develop more fulfilling, successful futures.

Between the three of us, we have a range of experience. I've worked in large technology organizations for the bulk of my career. Before joining IBM, I had brief stints in education and on Wall St. At IBM, I changed job every 18 months or so, for 16 years. I moved to Pitney Bowes, where I have worked as a VP DMT Europe Sales since 2016. Additionally, I love working with startups – hence I'm on the board of several. Carbon's Marine Aubin is a trailblazer for women in tech. The co-president of Girlz In Web, she is also a board member at the UN Women French Committee. Georgina Hill is a Junior Marketing Manager for a tech start-up. Bright and in tune with the upcoming generation of female leaders, she is keen to know what she and her contemporaries can do now to ensure a greater proportion make it to the top of the corporate ladder.

Why Carbon? It has always amazed me that the same element, carbon, can be found in two different forms today – either as the common graphite – or as a diamond. Although alchemists have had trouble changing lead into gold, mother nature has shown that with the right environment of pressure, heat and time she can turn graphite into diamonds. We too are diamonds in the making – all we need is the right environment in which to transform. We simply need to step out and shine!

Based on all the research I'd done, together with Marine and Georgina, we have created a programme designed to build women's self-belief, helping them to forge a personal brand that will support them to succeed. We call our method the '8 Cs', and I'll take a moment to introduce them to you. Each of the following chapters in this book takes one of our Cs as its subject and tells you exactly how to make it work for you.

Choice

The power of proactive choice is huge, but women often limit their choices unconsciously. Embracing positive choices and opening yourself to the huge potential your future holds is the first step.

Confidence

Confidence is something that's made, not born. We reframe the whole idea of confidence as something that emerges through practice. Developing rock-solid confidence is within your control – we show you how.

Character

Strong self-awareness, informed by an honest and positive appraisal of your best qualities, and an in-depth understanding of all aspects of your personality is an important precursor to confidence and clarity. In this chapter we help you identify the core values that matter most to you.

Clarity

Developing clarity of vision is the key to creating life goals that will help shape a path to a more fulfilling future. Our framework will help you execute those goals.

Consistency

Creating a personal brand that is consistent will build your colleagues' and employer's confidence in you. Consistent, conscientious delivery, based on clarity is a key leadership trait.

Change

The way you pursue, react to and adapt to change dictates so many aspects of your life. Seizing positive change with both hands puts you firmly in the driving seat.

Calm

Keeping a cool head is something that is an asset in any workplace situation. Start small by introducing a mindfulness practice for a few minutes a day. We share a calm for beginners practice to get you started.

Community

Tapping into a supportive community of women who share some of your core values and can empathize with the challenges you face is a great way to bolster confidence. It also opens your eyes to the choices available to you and enables you to share in the wisdom of women who have similar experiences.

Women have often asked me how I had the confidence to change career multiple times: from chemistry, to investment banking, to finance, to sales, to coaching and leadership. When I reflect on where this courage and confidence came from, the answer often surprises people. I know I was not born with it as I was always shy and timid as a child, and I know it was not a natural gift as it still terrifies me when I move. Rather, it has more in common with Malcolm Gladwell's theory: that 10,000 hours' practice at pretty much anything can turn you into an expert. For me, it was through failure that I discovered a powerful secret: Confidence is not innate – it is built through repeated practice, fed by a positive environment.

This confidence practice is something we must all do with ourselves, by volunteering to take on challenging projects, putting our hands up, by committing to keep going with aspects of our careers we find challenging until we get good at them.

But when it comes to creating workplace environments that nurture female talent, we can all help each other. Community networks of women encourage discussion across ranks, and a sense of shared interest; of looking out for one another.

NEW NETWORKS

Men have had these structures, of course, for years. They play golf, bond on corporate jollies to football or rugby matches, they belong to the same social clubs (although, thankfully, the old-fashioned gentlemen's clubs are increasingly a thing of the past). Men are more likely to be able to make evening dinners and events that female workers with families find more difficult to attend. It's at these informal semi-social meetings that men hear about opportunities, or glean useful insider information that will give them an advantage in their current job. These networks support the inadvertent gender bias that privileges men in the workplace. We women need to counter this by creating similar networks of our own. I think of it in terms of karma too: what goes around comes around. As women, in what is, particularly in senior corporate ranks, still a man's world, we need to say good things about one another behind each other's backs.

Women are more naturally inclined to collaborate than men. That's a fact borne out by countless research papers. In recent Canadian research by a co-working company, 76% of women said they would turn to co-working colleagues to help solve a work challenge, compared with only 54% of men. Female leaders are more likely to canvas opinion before they make a big decision, too.[5]

Let's turn this 'soft advantage' to serve ourselves and

---

5. www.gsb.columbia.edu/mygsb/faculty/research/pubfiles/4600/
GenderLeaderOverconfidence.pdf

build support networks that help to redress the balance. It's my passionate hope that Carbon Leadership will become one such network and that our 8 Cs method for building confidence, increasing clarity and improving the perception of choice for women in their careers, will catch on. We're excited to hear what you make of it, too.

Join the conversation.

twitter.com/carbon_leaders

www.carbonleadership.co

CHOICE

'One's philosophy is not best expressed in words; it is expressed in the choices one makes... and the choices we make are ultimately our responsibility.'
Eleanor Roosevelt

CHOICE. IT'S A SMALL word with huge power. Sadly, it's a power that many women feel they don't have. The right to choose, to alter our circumstances and define the shape of our lives. Without choice, we lose the ownership of and accountability for our actions. We become pawns in someone else's game.

For many women, living in societies where a woman's role is rigidly set, where freedoms are curtailed and daily economic realities ensure survival is the only priority, it's entirely understandable that the average woman would feel stymied at best, and utterly powerless at worst. She has very little choice about the shape of her life, unless she chooses to rebel (possibly risking her life in the process).

But for the rest of us? It's a pervasive myth, the product of a complicated mixture of social conditioning and learned 'female' behaviour, often reinforced by a work culture that, at a deep level, perpetuates the same story. This culture persists even when, at surface level, an organization may be doing all the right things to try to create a level playing field and encourage diversity (actively seeking to recruit more women, offering flexible working, offering mentoring).

In the corporate world I often come across individuals who believe they do not have a choice. 'I have to do this job', they say, or; 'Overtime is expected, they'll think I'm a slacker if I leave on time', or; 'I can't have this career if I want a family'. It seems like a fait accompli. We box ourselves into a corner under the misdirection of our own negative assumptions. I have often asked myself why this is the case. Is it as Isaiah Berlin, the famous Oxford professor says, 'Choices must be made, sometimes tragic losses accepted in the pursuit of some preferred ultimate end'?[6] Is it the tragedy of choice that stops us, that we are conditioned to believe that success always comes at a terrible price?

WORTH IT?

But what if the price isn't too terrible, and what's more, it's worth it? 'We need to move away from what I call the Wonder Woman syndrome,' says Carbon's Marine Aubin. 'When we look to role models such as Sheryl Sandberg and Hillary Clinton, we see the bright public figure, not the army behind them. We need to be realistic and not idealize what success looks like, because there's a danger that we imagine it to be exceptional and unattainable.'

---

6. Isaiah Berlin, *The Power of Ideas*

She's right. As women, we so often limit ourselves unthinkingly, partly in our fantasies about role models being exceptional. Of course, there's good old fear of failure thrown in to the mix too, looming large over women who struggle to find the gumption to ask for the things that might broaden their career possibilities (working on more high-profile projects, or being put forward for leadership training).

Perhaps women choose different paths to avoid embarrassment and the inevitable imposter syndrome that's the unwelcome side effect of being in an extreme minority. And we limit ourselves in advance too, anticipating how future needs (based around the children we may want someday) impact on the path our career takes.

In order to delve deeper into this subject, we at Carbon took 20 women who had potential, and worked with them one-to-one on what was stopping them from taking the next step. The results were fascinating. There was a certain degree of fear of failure, which did not surprise me at all. But what did surprise me was that in one way or another, they believed that if they were worthy, the opportunity would come to them at the right time in the right way. If it was 'meant to be', it would find its way to them in the future. Again, we came back to a lack of active choice, almost an accidental career path, that they'd find the right career path by a mixture of serendipity and patience. When I went to men in a similar situation what came out most was the lack of confidence in their abilities and a fear of public failure, but they were more likely to apply for the opportunity anyway, thinking, 'I'll throw my hat in or I'll miss my chance.' Men tend to be more lenient when they're assessing their own competence than women.

Women make such negative and self-limiting choices all the time without realizing that that's what they're doing. Many choices feel like non-options for women. But this in itself is a choice. It's a negative choice, but it's still a choice.

A MINDSET THAT STARTS EARLY

By the time women come into the workforce, years of habitual passivity make for an unwillingness to put themselves in a position where they may fail. An aversion to stepping up has become ingrained in their psyche. It's so deep, it's unconscious. Research by psychologist Carol Dweck from the 1980s looking at how bright girls and boys in the fifth grade approached new, confusing and challenging material, found that the higher a girl's IQ, the more likely she was to give up when she felt stumped.[7] She surmised this was perhaps because bright girls had been primed to believe that their cleverness was intrinsic, rather than something that could be improved on. They were quick to doubt their ability to face the challenge and give up. Boys, in contrast, were happier to keep working at the challenge, understanding they could develop their skills and abilities through practice. They found the new material challenging and were more likely to redouble their efforts than give up.

The boys were more accustomed to feedback that

---

7. Carol S. Dweck, *Self-theories: Their Role in Motivation, Personality, and Development* (Taylor & Francis, 2000)

encouraged them to persevere, she argued, whereas girls had been told they were 'clever'. This places hugely unhelpful cultural constraint around choice. In order to believe you have a choice in something requires a certain amount of positive self-assessment concerning the skills involved. In some instances, now disproven theories about boys being intrinsically better at maths (a consequence of better spatial awareness, according to the myth[8]) persist in the minds of teachers and parents.

'This passivity is built into social life too from a very early age,' says Carbon's Georgina Hill. 'Girls are supposed to wait for things to just "happen" to them. Wait for a boy to ask them out, wait for praise rather than asking for feedback, wait for a marriage proposal. Girls learn to live by the credo: "Good things come to those who wait." This is a recipe for dissatisfaction. In fact, good things come to those who seek them.'

The initial challenge we set our coaching clients is to make a mental shift from negative choices to positive ones. To move from 'I don't want' to 'I want.' In doing so, they resolve to make proactive choices that are motivated by their goals and priorities rather than passive 'negative choices' that are reactive and come from a place of habitual people-pleasing, underpinned with a toxic combination of inadequacy, fear and self-deprecation.

This passivity stands in stark contrast to the way women feel in home and family life, where they make the lion's share of decisions on children, holidays, major purchasing, what

---

8. www.newscientist.com/article/dn14026-exploding-the-myth-that-boys-are-better-at-maths/

to eat, and where to live. In a 2009 survey published in the Harvard Business Review, women were found to make 94% of household decisions on home furnishing and 60% of decisions on car purchasing.[9] Why is it that we don't feel we have the same jurisdiction in our offices as we do at home?

ONE WOMAN'S EPIPHANY

I'm going to share a story with you from my own career that demonstrates how deep this self-limiting habitual thinking can run and the unconventional strategies required to disrupt it.

Some years ago I had a brilliant personal assistant. She was one of the smartest people I'd ever met. Exceptionally capable and fantastic at her job. She was efficient, incisive, analytical and commercially minded and it was clear to me from the day that she started that she would be better suited to a more senior, strategic position. She was a single mother and had worked as a secretary for seven years.

After we had worked together for six months, a position came up in our marketing team. The salary was almost double her existing salary at the time.

I scheduled a meeting with her and suggested she apply. She was shocked and told me she was underqualified. She said she liked her job and was flattered by me thinking of her, but explained that she couldn't apply.

I took matters into my own hands and went to HR. I explained to them that I wanted to promote her into the

---

9. www.hbr.org/2009/09/the-female-economy

role. I explained that I would gradually lighten her secretarial workload and give her more of the tasks that related to the marketing job.

By the end of three months, she was doing the full job. I called her into a meeting again and asked her how she felt about having turned down the invitation to apply for the job. 'I'm so glad I didn't take it. I love my job now,' she said. I told her she'd been doing the job for months and explained that we had kept the extra salary aside for her. If she accepted the job, she could keep the arears.

She took it, but was in a state of shock, and still questioned my faith in her. She went on to have a very successful career in marketing, but she would probably still be stuck doing admin had she not had the opportunity forced on her. The marketing role didn't feel like a viable choice for her, even when it was offered to her!

SOUND FAMILIAR?

Stop for a moment and think about it. Have you ever sat back and stayed quiet in a meeting when you had plenty to say, then regretted it later? Or held back from suggesting a more inclusive activity when male colleagues arrange a golfing weekend with clients? Perhaps you have shied away from putting yourself forward for high-profile projects or volunteering to speak internally or at industry events because 'that's not my thing.'

Of course, there may be more obvious, bigger-picture examples too: projecting into a series of future what-ifs when you're debating an exciting job abroad then turning it down; playing down a big commercial win by saying: 'It was all down to the team,' or 'I was in the right place at the right time.' Most men wouldn't behave this way. They would absorb the accolades, feel pleased with the plaudits, let the back-slapping buoy them along. They'd feel great about it.

When women are praised, they may often feel a sense of imposter syndrome, a suspicion that they don't really deserve the positive feedback. What's more, there's a nasty cultural myth that there's something unseemly about being perceived as 'pleased with yourself'. Self-deprecation is the consequent go-to response. But it's far more damaging than it seems. You're saying: 'It wasn't just me…' Or: 'Really, anyone could have done it,' and your subconscious takes this in – it becomes self-fulfilling. The more you fall back on this brush-off, the more you start to believe it and the more it erodes your confidence and sense of personal agency.

Having carved out a successful career in tech innovation and having worked as a product and innovation manager for a range of digital businesses, Carbon's Marine Aubin recently launched her own consultancy firm. But despite her impressive resume, she has had to train herself to adjust her mindset from one that constantly cast her as unworthy and inadequate: 'When I was 25, I always looked up at the career of people who were 35,' she says. 'I set very high goals for myself and although I did well, I never took the time to congratulate myself before moving on to the next challenge. I had the impression that I was an under-achiever when I had already achieved much more than many people.'

Although Marine is conscious of this inbuilt self-doubt, it still surfaces: 'I launched my own business as a consultant recently, and I was terrified I wouldn't have any clients, even though I have a very qualitative network and had at least two meetings with CxOs of large corporations booked in… and three job offers. Within a month of setting up I had signed a five-month deal with a client that guaranteed me a monthly wage. Now I'm feeling more confident about my decisions and cutting myself some slack. The voice of self-doubt is still there, but through persistently proving it wrong, I'm strengthening my self-belief, one step at a time.'

IMPOSTER SYNDROME SURFACES AGAIN

That self-belief eludes so many talented women is shocking. Carbon's Georgina Hill experienced exactly the same thing when she started in her first job at a start-up last year: 'Starting my current job fresh out of university and getting much more responsibility than I expected, I was hit by a huge dose of imposter syndrome. I constantly vented to my mother, sister and friends about my worries that I was going to be discovered, and found incapable. I know I'm capable and have the skills, but I still don't really feel I deserve to be here. I'm working on it, but the unsettling doubt is always there.'

The American self-help guru Tony Robbins recommends the following exercise to anyone who suffers from this internal naysaying. It's simple but incredibly powerful. When I tried it for myself, I was shocked by the way that my internal monologue limits my choices on a daily basis. Robbins recommends noting down the 'self-talk' that runs through your mind for a whole day. Keep a notepad on your person or jot down the thoughts on your phone.

I did this on an average work day. Here's a list of some of the things that were running through my head:

'Why did I forget to exercise again? I'm so lazy.'

'Will he leave me if I get fat?'

'Sandwiches again – why can't I be one of those moms who has healthy food for her kids for lunch?'

'Big meeting today. Hope I don't screw it up!'

'I wonder what he needs to talk to me about? I hope I'm not getting fired.'

Looking at all this self-directed vitriol in black and white was sobering and horrifying. Had a third party directed any of these nasty, belittling and unkind thoughts towards my daughter, say, I'd have clobbered them. But this was the internal monologue that was babbling away inside my own head.

Contrast this with the CEO of GE, Jeff Immelt, who spoke at a Harvard Interview, which I heard relayed by Professor Michael L Tushman of Harvard Business School, who says that no matter how stressful and problematic the previous day was, he always starts a new day by staring into his own reflection and saying, 'Hello, handsome'. This might make you laugh (as it did me), but it has a serious benefit, and it's certainly a powerful indicator of positive self-esteem. Can you imagine any woman you know looking at herself in the mirror, first thing in the morning, and saying: 'Hello, beautiful'? Thought not. After Professor Tushman had spoken, the head of HR at PB got up to speak, and made reference to it. She said she was going to channel Jeff Immelt's trick in future: 'I probably won't say "Hello, beautiful", but "Hello, not-so-bad might be a good start…"'

Everybody laughed. It was self-deprecating, but NOT true. It spoke to the differences between men and women, but these are differences that don't always serve us well.

THE TYRANNY OF LIKEABILITY

It's this deep-seated desire to be *liked,* a product of early social conditioning, that so often holds women back at work. It means we find it incredibly difficult to say no. It feels wrong to choose our own needs over the needs of a boss, or a colleague. We're built to cooperate, collaborate and support, but many women fall into a trap of *only* doing these things to the detriment of their careers. It's partly because once you get a reputation for saying 'Yes' to demands from colleagues, they ask you for more and more favours.

It's self-perpetuating and whilst it may sometimes throw up a fresh opportunity you may not have considered, it could also distract you from your own priorities and goals. The horrible irony is that the more you say 'Yes', the less they'll appreciate it. In the same way that being a doormat for a partner is detrimental to your own needs, being too willing to accommodate your colleagues' needs at work means you get taken for granted. In the long run, you won't even get the same likeability pay-off.

Think about the choices you make about the way you spend your time on a daily basis. How much of your time do you spend as you intended to at the beginning of the day? How much time do you spend doing things for yourself? When it comes to trying to reset the balance on this front, it's the instinctive, unthinking choices we make that are potentially the most insidious and hardest to challenge.

This instinctive thinking isn't only limited by the unhelpful habit of putting other people's needs before your own. It may also be informed by an old-fashioned view of choice itself.

Many of us, men and women alike, have got stuck in an unhealthily binary way of thinking about choice, particularly when it comes to weighing up the right balance between work and family life. We think in terms of either/or, assuming 'balance' is something to strive for at a set point in time, like finding the sweet spot between hot and cold in the shower. But just like the perfect temperature, it proves eternally elusive. However, if we broaden the definition and accept that 'balance' is something that can only really be judged over the context of a decade rather than an average week, we can step back and get a lot more perspective on it.

BALANCE: A LONG-TERM VIEW

We can't 'have it all' at every moment. But we certainly can over a lifetime. I think one of the best quotes I have ever heard was from IBM's Michele Stern, leader of the IBM North America One Channel team. 'Remember you can have it all, but just not at the same time.' This is an incredibly powerful statement – it takes the pressure off being perfect all the time. Careers run in phases, and modern workplaces are increasingly developing a more flexible approach to career management. A linear ladder-climbing trajectory is only one of many options. It's reflective of the fact that for many workers, a choice that's right for now won't necessarily be the right one in three years' time. Ladders have begun to look old-fashioned. We'd do better to think of career paths as more of a web, or as Sheryl Sandberg calls it, a 'jungle gym'.

To help you think about the possibilities open to you at this exact moment, try the following exercise. It's designed to help you unpick the reasoning that many of us use to talk ourselves out of life-changing decisions. Uncertainty about whether to embrace a new choice is often governed by your perception of the risk on either side, so this simple questionnaire gives you a way of structuring this thought process, weighing up the pros and the cons in an impartial way. By assigning a numeric value to each of the outcomes, you'll get a more accurate snapshot of the choice itself.

EXERCISE:

1. Ask yourself a very good question often raised by the Lean In organization: 'What would you do if you weren't afraid?'

2. Take a blank sheet and draw a line in the middle.

3. On the left part write down every anxiety you have in mind about what could go wrong or impact on your life negatively if you were to take the plunge.

4. On the right-hand side, write down every anxiety you have about what might happen if you don't do it.

5. Once you have your two lists, rate each risk on both

sides giving them a score out of five for likelihood and a second score out of five for the likely scale of the negative impact on your life. Once you have your scores, add the impact to the likelihood so that you have a single score for each risk.

6. Total up your pros and cons, and see which has smaller figure (the least negative impact on your life overall). That's the choice you should go for.

7. If you go for it, make an action plan with very small steps. If the next step looks too scary, it means you need to break it down into smaller steps. If you decide not to go for it, you've made a positive choice not to pursue something because you've done some life math on it.

Example: Take a job in another company

○ **Risks if I do it**
  • Losing my current wage
  • Losing my stability and comfort
  • Working in a new environment I know nothing about
  • Losing my good relationship with some coworkers

RISK – TO DO	L	I	T	RISK – NOT TO DO	L	I	T
Losing my current wage	5	3	15	Feeling more and more unhappy with my current position	5	5	25
Losing my stability and comfort	5	2	10	Feeling low, even when not at work	4	5	20
An unfamiliar workplace and environment	5	1	5	Losing an opportunity for career jump	4	4	16
Losing strong relationships with coworkers	4	3	12	Losing opportunity to grow as a person	5	3	15
TOTAL RISK			42	TOTAL RISK			76
L = LIKELIHOOD I = IMPACT T = TOTAL							

○ **Risks if I don't**
- Feeling more and more unhappy with my position
- Feeling more and more low, even when not at work
- Losing an opportunity to make the career jump I want

○ **Action plan**
- Updating my resume
- Looking at some job offers I'd like to apply for
- Updating my LinkedIn profile
- Applying for a job I don't really want and using it to develop key skills

- Going to a networking event with some people who could be interested in my profile
- Sending a follow-up email to the people I met at the networking event to let them know I'm looking for a new opportunity
- Applying for a job I'd really like to have

Fill in the chart yourself and evaluate your risks and the personal effect it will have on your life. If you decide to make the leap, draw up an action plan to prepare for broken-down baby steps to ease you towards your choice.

A colleague of mine, a senior executive in a major tech organization, who has had a varied and hugely successful career says this analogy resonates with her. 'The definition of success and happiness changes over time. I know mine has. Career accomplishment and family were my absolute focus when my children were young; social life and friendships or leisure and charitable pursuits were deprioritized for a later time in life. Today, friendships and charitable give-back are centre stage, and around the corner I can see leisure pursuits knocking on the door to join the mix.'

TOO MUCH CHOICE?

On the flip side, but equally problematic to the 'I have no choice' mindset, is a paralysing and overwhelming sense of endless possibility. Too much choice can feel mind-boggling and lead to similar inertia. In another everyday arena, grocery shopping, big businesses such as Tesco in the UK have recently made a choice to reduce the number of products they offer. The chief executive of Tesco, Dave Lewis, made a radical decision to remove 30,000 lines from the shelves of his stores, recognizing that too much choice can, counter-intuitively, have a negative impact on profits. When they are faced with too many decisions and possibilities, shoppers buy less, not more. It's the same with careers.

Narrowing choices on some things that become major time wasters (what to wear, for example) can help free up time for choices that are important. Marine Aubin says she plans her meals and outfits in advance. 'I remember reading that President Obama planned his suits ahead for the whole week so he could focus on decision making. I always wear the same skirt with same top and same shoes and dresses together so I don't waste my brain energy during the week on unimportant choices.'

Barry Schwartz, a psychologist who wrote *The Paradox of Choice,* says that the more options on offer, the less likely we are to be satisfied with our choices. The sense of 'should've, could've' possibilities sets the scene for post-choice ennui. 'It's received wisdom that the more choice we have, the greater freedom we have, and that more choice is a good thing,' he says in his TED talk on the same topic, which has had almost ten million hits. 'But too much choice causes paralysis. In a study on investments in voluntary retirement funds, for every ten mutual funds an employer offered, they saw a 2% reduction in the number of staff signed up for them. The more funds on offer, the fewer people took them up. As a result, they missed out on employer contributions to their pension. When there are lots of alternatives to consider there are lots of ways to retrospectively imagine positive attributes of all the choices you didn't opt for. The net result is less satisfaction.'

In conclusion he says: 'There's no doubt that some choice is better than none, but it doesn't follow that the more choice you have the better off you are.' When it comes to planning a career, you need to do the work of identifying the choices most suited to you without getting distracted by thinking your way along unhelpful and unlikely tangents that may distract rather than focus you.

The lure of retraining is particularly strong post motherhood, particularly for women who are working in male-dominated industries where long hours are the norm. Sometimes retraining is a brilliant decision – a refreshing and exciting opportunity to start afresh and use your unique set of skills in a new way. You may end up with a more fulfilling career as a result, even if it necessitates stepping off the part of the 'jungle gym' you're on and going back to the ground floor of another part of the frame.

Sometimes, though, women opt to retrain because they feel like their existing career path has come to a dead end, or because they feel that stepping back from a full-time position will mean less satisfying work where they get sidelined and passed over. They worry they'll get 'Mommy-tracked' as one Harvard Business School alumni put it in an eye-opening piece of research that analysed the career paths of three generations of HBS graduates.

It's hard to make a positive choice when you don't like any of the ones that are obviously on offer. When there's no precedent for the choice you want to make (say you want greater flexibility without sacrificing status and future career prospects), it isn't surprising that so many women do a sideways jump, step off the ladder to set up businesses on their own, or choose to retrain in a different career altogether.

LACK OF ROLE MODELS

When I was looking for a mentor at IBM, this problem of precedent became apparent. I wanted to find a woman who was like me: somebody who worked full time, had a partner who also worked in an equally demanding job and had children. I was hoping for a hack – advice on how to manoeuvre within a large organization like IBM; a mentor to advise me on how best to progress without losing my sense of balance. There were plenty of helpful and inspiring men around, but I wanted a female mentor as I felt I would be able to connect more easily with a woman. Someone who would intuitively understand my perspective. I wanted her advice on best practice – figuring she'd be able to offer invaluable advice that would help me to get on.

It was tricky to find someone who had a similar career to the one I hoped for, and whose home situation matched my own. My senior manager matched me up with a couple of women in the firm who they hoped might fit the bill, but the first had a partner who didn't work and the second had a nanny and a partner in a far more flexible job. It was a stark reminder of the fact that the choice I had made was one without much of a precedent. In the end, I found someone myself: Michele Stern. She showed me that when you take the pressure of being perfect off the table and measure yourself through the history of your career rather than a moment in time you will be in awe of what you have accomplished.

It's clear that we need to open our minds on choice, to think more laterally and imaginatively about it. Most of all, we need to remember we have a choice – in any given moment. We mustn't sit back and wait for opportunities to present themselves. Being proactive is the key to active choice. As the famous pilot, Elinor Smith once said: 'It (came) to my attention that people of accomplishment rarely sat back and let things happen to them. They went out and happened to things.'

CONFIDENCE

*'Confidence is preparation. Everything else
is beyond your control.'*
Richard Kline

TO DO

Endless column inches and whole swathes of self-help sections of bookshops have been devoted to the holy grail of self-development: confidence. It's commonly accepted that when it comes to positive self-regard, women struggle more than men.

Partly, I believe, the reason that this stream of material shows no sign of ever slowing is that our concept of confidence, the way we understand it (and the general received psychological wisdom around it), is unhelpful. I think this also has a lot to do with the reason women struggle so much with developing confidence.

The standard dictionary definition tells us that confidence is: 'The feeling or belief that one can have faith in or rely on someone or something.' Therefore, we surmise, self-confidence is an intrinsic thing, a 'faith', or belief in yourself that sets it apart from reason. It's something you either have or you don't.

If this were true, I would be a lost cause. Growing up with an archetypal 'tiger mom', I was barely ever praised and was not taught to develop an innate sense of self-worth. Thankfully, I did have some wonderful alternative role models in my life who were encouraging and loving and gave me what my mother couldn't. Of course my mother loved me, but her way of showing that love was to push me, to make sure I never rested on my laurels, not for a moment, always nudging me to wonder why I hadn't done better still.

Despite the fact that this made me extremely self-critical and trapped in a negative feedback loop where I was desperate for her approval but never got it, her approach had an unexpected side-effect.

CONFIDENCE THROUGH COMPETENCE

I learnt to build confidence out of competence. Through perseverance and practice, I grafted my way to become more and more proficient at a whole range of things. And this proficiency, whether it was in debates, in the mathematics classroom, or in the swimming pool, led me to develop a powerful confidence in my own ability to tackle pretty much anything I set my mind to. In this way, I came to view confidence as an active thing. Something to be practised. A process rather than a destination.

I'll give you a specific example. When I was at high school, my mother signed me up for the debating society. At 15, I was a shy child, wary of drawing attention to myself.

In class, I worked hard, but kept my head down. I was reluctant (to say the least) about going to an after-school club that necessitated standing up in front of other students and arguing a point. After my first semester in the society, I went to an inter-school competition, along with the rest of the students in the club. I will never forget the heart-sink I felt when the results came back. I had been ranked last out of 473 students – LAST. My mother was angry on my behalf, and confronted the teacher who ran the debating society in my school, saying: 'She needs more practice.' She made it clear to me that I would keep going, and that she expected me to practise and improve.

I kept on with it and over a number of years gained more and more confidence in debating. I began to win competitions and became more assertive in class. Eventually, I got so proficient at debating that I was chosen to represent Canada in a major international competition. It was a powerful lesson in perseverance and confidence building and it has stayed with me. With tenacity and application, I truly believe that most people can accomplish almost anything. But you must be proactive and not concede defeat when a challenge feels tough.

Then my confidence was really put to the test when I was asked to do a TEDx by Delphine Poucet. I was very excited by the prospect. I loved the idea of telling people that I had done a TEDx talk – but I realized, like Tim Urban said in his talk, I liked it after the fact! I liked crossing it off my bucket list – the actual writing and pre-talk stress and sweaty palms brought back memories of my ninth grade debate!

As we drew near the date and the deliverables – the

notion did cross my mind of cancelling my participation, I'm ashamed to admit – but when I talked about this my son Qaahir said: 'Well you can choose to quit or you can choose to try.' He quoted me to me! Now, my son is a teenager and quite reserved, so most of the time I think that whatever I tell him may be going in one ear and out the other – but he hears every word – so take it from me do not dish out advice to your kids that you cannot take yourself! Well, obviously I was not going to be a quitter. I did do it and it was one of the best experiences I have ever had!

We talked a little in the choice chapter about the way girls are conditioned to view choice as a passive thing. We normalize this passivity. It impacts on our narratives about our lives, the way we view our careers up until now and our prospects for the future. You're more likely to hear a woman say: 'It wasn't meant to be', when they miss out on a job opportunity, or: 'Right place, right time. I was lucky', when things go their way. I often used to call myself an 'accidental success'.

This passive way of looking at life does nothing for your confidence. You are never the rainmaker in this scenario. Success, or failure, just happens to you.

Flip this and claim ownership of that success or failure and you're immediately in more of an assertive position. This boosts confidence as it's empowering. Rather than viewing confidence as something that has a set point, it becomes a quality you can consciously work to enhance. By taking responsibility for your performance, you commit to being the architect of your future.

Being honest about your weaknesses, and taking the rap when something goes wrong, also shows strength of character and self-awareness. Both traits that are desirable in leaders. An ego that is so fragile that you can't countenance acknowledgement of your own imperfections and areas for improvement rings serious warning bells for anyone wanting to enter senior management. There is always room for improvement in virtually every area of competency and expertise, for anyone.

When I read *Outliers* by Malcolm Gladwell, it really resonated with me. His theory, that: 'Ten thousand hours is the magic number of greatness' was the conclusion of exhaustive research into world-class athletes, musicians and tech superstars. He wasn't saying that anyone could become a superstar with 10,000 hours of practice, but that anyone could become expert in that time. As a side effect, some would unleash their genius once they'd put in the hours too: 'Natural ability requires a huge investment of time to be made manifest,' he explained in a subsequent interview after a huge backlash had followed the viral spread of his soundbite (an oversimplification of his argument).

It's my belief that confidence also, as well as expertise, emerges as a result of consistent practice. It doesn't magically appear, like a reward after a certain amount of time. Rather, it is forged through a process. As you work on yourself and fine-tune your performance, you learn new things and adapt to a range of challenges. Through these experiences, confidence grows.

Another interesting point Gladwell makes is about how students spend their summer holidays. As a broad generalization, students who are stuck at home, with a lot of screen time and little stimulation 'go backwards' over the summer break. Whilst it might be relaxing, it also means that the skills students have been working on during term time: numeracy, literacy, creative thinking as well as sports, music and art, lie dormant during the holiday. In contrast, as a general rule, children who have parents with the time and budget to experience new cultures and environments, and pay for extra-curricular sports clubs, music camps and visits to cultural institutions during the summer break, return to school in September at an equivalent or improved standard. They get far more stimulation.

COMMIT TO SELF-IMPROVEMENT

This translates into 'practice' – developing and enriching a whole range of skills and broadening experience and knowledge. In the same way as parents do for children, we all have a duty to nurture ourselves. Take yourself out of context regularly, head to museums and galleries; read interesting material that falls outside your area of expertise; sign up for workplace training that builds on your skills. Watch TED talks. Seek out anything that might give you a fresh perspective. If there's something you want to get better at, keep at it.

Of course, although 10,000 hours may be the benchmark for excellence, a significantly smaller number of hours may be all that's required to get good at something. It's possible to make major improvements in only 100 hours. Look at newby marathon runners. They may never have run long distance before, but with dedication and application, they can turn in a decent time with four to six months of training. As they work on their form, fitness and endurance, their body adapts to the new regime. Their lean muscle mass increases and their lung capacity improves. Their heart rate drops and their blood pressure is reduced. They become calmer, and are less likely to suffer from low mood, which has a knock-on impact on the rest of their lives.

The vast majority of these runners won't suddenly become club-standard competitors, they aren't 'experts' in any sense, but they are competent and will have developed a newfound confidence in their bodies.

Long-distance running is a great example of something that many people come to in middle age. We think nothing of a 40-something running an endurance race for the first time. But when it comes to developing more obviously work-related skills, we assume training is something that happens early on in a career. We aren't accustomed to the idea of on-the-job retraining, of dramatically changing tack without going back to college.

I had to challenge my own anxieties around this when I switched from finance to sales in my late 30s. I had carved out a successful career in finance, working my way up to CFO level. But I had always wanted to work in a more commercial role. When an exciting opportunity arose – a senior job in sales – and I was headhunted for it internally (in truth it was somewhat forced on me) I knew I had to go for it. But I also knew I had no real sales experience. To bridge the gap, I spent some time shadowing people in similar roles and did a stint of cold-calling myself, practising my script on low-level contacts until I got comfortable with it and felt I understood what it took to make a sale at a grass-roots level. It was empowering, and more useful than a term spent in a classroom learning about the theory of selling. I was able to add experiential understanding of selling to my tool belt.

We all need to get comfortable with the idea that learning is something that happens throughout our career. Our work paths are not linear in the way they once were. They twist and turn; there are hops sideways and jumps forwards, and sometimes huge U-turns. We need to adapt and adopt a flexible mindset to enable us to override anxieties we may feel about our lack of expertise or unpreparedness for new challenges. We need to be able to roll with changes, be willing to stick our hands up and say: 'I'm not an expert in X but I'm willing to learn and practise.' In short, we need to learn how to learn.

This is something that comes more naturally to men than women. To return to the Hewlett Packard research we touched on in the introduction, men are more inclined to take a leap of faith and put themselves forward for opportunities they aren't, on paper, qualified for. Women expect to meet close to 100% of the criteria before they apply. It is so important to let go of this hang-up.

One way to get more comfortable with this idea of stretching yourself, taking calculated risks and striking out more is to take on pet projects that straddle different domains. It's a great way to test out potential areas for development. When I mentor, I always recommend that non-creatives take on a creative project. Volunteering to consult on or contribute to a project that's slightly outside of your usual remit is also a great idea.

Confidence that grows out of competence runs deep. Look around you at work and in your personal life and think about the people who have true confidence. It's unlikely they will be the ones who talk a lot in meetings, or dominate conversations at work by drawing attention to their achievements. They don't need to big themselves up and they actively go out of their way to share the limelight with colleagues and collaborators.

GETTING COMFORTABLE WITH CONFIDENCE

This is what sets confidence apart from arrogance. We often confuse the two, which can lead women, in particular, with our intrinsic desire to be liked, to shy away from being perceived as confident, or 'full of' ourselves. But when we reappraise confidence and begin to regard it, accurately, as the best way to underpin a humble and collaborative approach to teamwork, it starts to look like more of an appealing trait. When you're secure in your own capability, flexibility and resilience, it breeds humility, rather than arrogance.

But deep confidence is so lacking in many young women today. Many suffer from terrible imposter syndrome, or rather 'Imposter experience', as Professor Pauline Rose Clance, then of Georgia State University, has retrospectively re-named it (she did the original research on the phenomenon in the '70s). What's fascinating is that despite imposter syndrome being seized on by various feminist theorists as a partial explanation for women's lack of advancement in the workplace, it has since been reappraised. Clance wrote in 2003 that she had adjusted her theory and accepts that men are just as likely as women to experience feelings of inadequacy and unworthiness at work. The mystery remains: why is it that women seem to heed these feelings more than men, and self-limit because of them? Psychologists have answered this in part by looking at the impact of early gender stereotyping, lessons that get internalized about what it means to be 'nice' girl.

There's a famous paradox known as the Dunning-Kruger effect (named after the Cornell psychologists who discovered it). In their research, they looked at the tendency of some people to overestimate their abilities. This seems to run contrary to Clance's research on imposter syndrome, but in fact,the picture is far more complex, as they found that high-ability individuals were comparatively more likely to underestimate their skill. In short, they discovered that the less competent people were, the more they overestimated their abilities. At its apex, this leads to a Trump-esque egotism. It's a helpful counter perspective to bear in mind next time you're faced with an alpha male with rock-solid confidence in his own abilities.

Although highly skilled men may suffer feelings of unworthiness, the margin by which they underestimate themselves seems to be far narrower. In a subsequent study from 2003, David Dunning worked with psychologist Joyce Ehrlinger at Washington State university to explore the relationship between confidence and competence in women. They gave students – a mixture of men and women – a quiz on scientific reasoning. Before they answered the questions, Dunning and Ehrlinger asked the students to rate their scientific competence, asking them the question 'Are you good at science?' The women rated themselves more negatively than the men – an average of 6.5 on a scale of 1–10 compared with 7.6 for the men. Then, after the quiz, when they were asked how well they had answered the questions, the women guessed they had got 5.8 out of 10 questions right, whilst the men guessed 7.1. The actual results were an average of 7.5 correct answers for women and 7.9 for the men. Take a moment and think about when you sold yourself short – it happens more often than you think!

Despite my success, I still suffer considerably with imposter syndrome. Every time I get called into a meeting unexpectedly with my boss, I have a sneaking suspicion I may be about to be sacked. I've come to accept that this anxiety is part of who I am, and I'm better at keeping it in check, but it's a clear indicator of its power that I still feel it so acutely.

FINDING YOUR CHEERLEADERS

One of the most effective antidotes to wobbly self-confidence is to find cheerleaders – people in your life who offer you unconditional positive regard. I borrow Kevin Carol's term for these people: 'CEOs – Chief Encouragement Officers.' These often turn out to be different from the people you expect them to be (i.e. parent and best friends). In my own case, I have been fortunate to have a few of these. My first and most formative was my nanny, Bella. She moved with me to Canada from Dar Es Salam.

Bella always made me feel as if I could achieve anything I wanted to. She was incredibly loving and taught me some self-care habits that have become life-long sanity savers. Every morning when I looked at myself in the mirror, she encouraged me to make a habit of saying out loud three things I liked about myself. Sometimes these were seemingly small and insignificant – my hands or the fact I'd aced a maths test. At other times, the things I noticed were more general things about my personality or things I'd managed to overcome – my perseverance with learning English and finally being able to read Shakespeare, or letting my sister have first pick at presents on birthdays (we shared a birthday). Whenever I remember, I still try to do this every day and I have encouraged my children to adopt the same habit.

My next CEO was my high school maths teacher, Mr Nguyen. Despite the fact that he had fairly poor English and spoke in simple sentences, he had a profound impact on my confidence. He constantly encouraged me, without judgement, and he always had my back, even when the criticism I suffered at home was working to do the opposite. When I graduated, he asked me to choose between two awards: valedictorian and most successful student ever (the Lieutenant Governor's award). As the latter was the more unusual, one-off award and I wasn't allowed to accept both, I chose that one. It was a great honour, and I felt really proud of my achievement. I had also been accepted into several Ivy League schools. It was a time to celebrate. After the ceremony, despite the fact that all the other parents and many teachers were congratulating her, my mother was upset that I had not won the valedictorian.

Mr Nguyen quietly took her to one side and said: 'You must recognize that this is the time for quiet pride, to celebrate your remarkable daughter's achievement and accept this wonderful gift.'

Now I'm a grown up, my number one CEO may surprise you. Rather than being a friend or trusted colleague, it is my daughter, Aliya. She has the most incredible faith in me, a belief that I can do anything I set my mind to. In fact if she sees me even thinking of a negative thought she pounces on it and replaces it with a positive one!

Friends often (but not always) have more of an agenda, with praise that runs 'That's great, but...' or 'That'll only work if...' This can be useful, but it isn't what you need from a CEO. You need unconditional positive regard. To pick an analogy my daughter would approve of, the best comparison for this is the Patronus Charm in Harry Potter. In order to conjure a protective spirit, a wizard must tap into a positive, happy memory. It's a skill that improves with practice, this summoning. A brief chat with a CEO can be just the catalyst you need to make it happen, to give you that sense that 'I can do this.'

To find a CEO it is best to be one to someone too. I had an incredibly bright mentee named Berna Sogut whom I wanted to sponsor in her career. In order to do this, I gave her a public challenge to try to get a meeting with the CxO of several cloud service providers who in general did not give the time of day to IBM. In a normal situation, had I gone the traditional route with a more seasoned seller this would have taken about three months to get – Berna, by using social media, got it done in a week. Fast forward a few months and we signed the biggest sale of Linux Power machines. When we were getting the accolades, I would encourage Berna to teach and show people how she managed this. She got noticed and promoted and she's thrilled. When asked how she felt about it she said something quite interesting: 'I will never forget what you did for me,

Shemin. I think it can make such a difference that now I'm trying to do the same for new interns and employees.'

Having a CEO is great. Being one is even better!

BE YOUR OWN ADVOCATE

For those times when you don't have a CEO to turn to, having affirmations you can call on will ensure you can act as a cheerleader for yourself. Affirmations will thrive when you remind yourself constantly to think positive thoughts about yourself. Author and self-help guru, Louise L. Hay says: 'The secret to having your affirmations work quickly and consistently is to prepare an atmosphere for them to grow in. Affirmations are like seeds planted in soil. Poor soil, poor growth. Rich soil, abundant growth. The more you choose to think thoughts that make you feel good, the quicker the affirmations work.'

And if you're feeling sceptical about the idea, research from Carnegie Mellon University may change your mind. A study by researchers there provides evidence that regular use of affirmations can protect against the damaging effects of stress on problem-solving performance. We are as we think.

Confidence feeds a virtuous cycle, too, and with every positive revolution it gets stronger. Active choices followed by consistent practice to gain confidence result in positive self-affirmation (hopefully bolstered by employer affirmation and CEO encouragement). All of this creates positive momentum to spur us on to make new positive choices, so the cycle begins again.

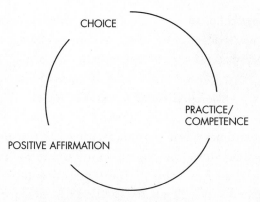

Figure 1: The Virtuous Cycle of Confidence

AN ENVIRONMENT THAT FEEDS CONFIDENCE

The final part of the puzzle is the trickiest to get right. In order to build true confidence, it's crucial that women seek out working environments, relationships and situations that nurture them. We need to get better at recognizing what 'good' looks like and moving towards it. We should feel happy, challenged and inspired at work. When we think about it, our main response should be positive.

I have a personal checklist that I use to assess how positive my workplace is (I use it as a series of deal-breakers when I'm considering a new job too). Here's what it says:

Do I/Will I like my immediate manager?

Do I/Will I look forward to coming into work?

Have I noticed any swearing or aggression in the workplace? Are people calm and non-aggressive?

Any evidence of bullying is a symptom of a toxic culture.

Have I noticed a lot of sarcasm, eye-rolling or

underlying contempt for the job, or for colleagues from members of my team?

How does my body feel when I step into my office?

I'm a big believer in trusting my gut, literally.

(When considering a new job) What do the people who work for my future boss have to say about their experience of working for him/her and being a part of the company?

I often ask to have coffee with a couple of employees before I decide on whether to take a job. As a general rule, when I request this meeting, a new department, or company I'm considering will send me two of their best people. I can tell straight away if we will get on and work well together.

I've turned down some great positions because I felt in my gut that I wouldn't be happy in them. Likewise, I took a major pay cut because I knew I'd really love working with a particular team and because I believed in the company.

Sometimes it isn't possible to be completely black and white. When you need to take a job for financial reasons, preparing yourself mentally for the fact that it may be out of step with your values is crucial. View it as a necessary but temporary move, and ultimately, a stepping stone to increased stability or the next part of your career.

Good team dynamics go a long way to create an environment where you can flourish. I know this myself from my experience as a manager. When I'm trying to gather ideas on a project from a team, I know that I get far more inspiration from people when they feel validated and don't worry about being judged. Often, I ask team members to write their ideas on a particular topic down on Post-it notes to bring to a meeting, then I stick them all up on a chart. This works better than asking people to shout out ideas verbally, as team members who aren't naturally extroverted and confident are likely to find this tricky and may just stay quiet. Think about your own workplace and the way you do things. Are there changes that could help to create more of a climate of confidence? What are they and how could you go about suggesting them to your boss?

PROJECTING CONFIDENCE

The American self-help coach Tony Robbins says that if you want to project an impression of confidence, you have to like yourself. You have to want to be you, and feel good in your skin. I think this is hard to argue with. In recent years, a new term for this positive self-regard has sprung up: self-compassion. It's a quality that enables you to cut yourself some slack, to see yourself in perspective rather than homing in on mistakes and negative aspects of yourself. People with high self-compassion extend the same kindness to themselves as they do to other people, and research shows that it can have a positive impact on a wide range of health-promoting behaviours.[10] These include safeguarding you from depression and anxiety, and preventing negative behaviours such as procrastination. When you like yourself, it's easier to find the confidence

---

10. www.psycnet.apa.org/psycinfo/2014-38834-001

to just do it.

Monitor your thoughts (try the exercise I mentioned where you record your self-talk), and try to match every negative thought with three positive ones. In *The God of Small Things* Arundhati Roy writes:

'A cold moth with unusually dense dorsal tufts landed lightly on Rahel's heart. Where its icy legs touched her, she got goosebumps. Six goosebumps on her careless heart. A little less her Ammu loved her.'

I like the way this speaks to the barely perceptible, but nonetheless powerful way negative comments can erode self-esteem. I always try to remember this with my staff and when I'm parenting, but it's far harder to police negativity that's directed towards yourself. But it's important to remember that negative and positive thoughts can't co-exist in the same moment.

If you struggle to let go of negative thoughts, meditation can really help you to develop a more mindful approach.

For some people, there's a residual (unhelpful) sense that you have to be broken down in order to be built back up. In some parts of the world, this underpins the education system, and even though it might be unfashionable and regarded as unhelpfully old-school elsewhere, it's an ethos that survives in certain corners of education and parenting theory. The 'tiger parent' craze is the latest manifestation of this. I think this is dangerous. Recent research has shown that this type of critical parenting may lead to academic success, but it comes at a high price – it compromises the self-esteem of children and impacts on their abilities to form positive relationships.[11]

If you have been the product of this type of parenting, the best thing you can do to build up your own confidence is to adopt a more compassionate view of yourself, and to return again and again to your competence and ability to learn, adapt and grow.

It's something I still struggle with, despite working on my confidence for years. In the past, I've been concerned about being labelled 'pushy' or 'difficult' at work. But over time, I've got better at asserting myself. I was recently in a meeting where there were a number of other staff present. I had a heated debate with a senior male member of staff – more senior in terms of years. I stood my ground, but felt uncomfortable. In the end the outcome of our debate was positive. I didn't think too much about it afterwards as I've got used to fighting my corner in meetings, even when there's an audience. However, other women who had been present said afterwards they felt that the way he had spoken to me had been aggressive. They fed this back to him, and he apologized to me. I accepted his apology and felt better for it, but I would have been fine without it.

A few years ago, this wouldn't have been the case, so I can see that my commitment to practising confidence is paying off. It's a lifelong project, as it is for most women.

Remind yourself, always, that confidence is made, not born. It's within your control.

---

11. www.time.com/88125/the-tiger-mom-effect-is-real-says-large-study/

CHARACTER

'Your character will be what you
yourself choose to make it.'
John Lubbock

WHAT DO I MEAN by character? It's a combination of your personality and your core values: the things that really matter to you. Character is built over time, shaped by your experiences, your prejudices and your habits. It's constantly changing and evolving to accommodate new information, influences and shifts in perspective.

It's important to check in with this changing aspect of yourself regularly. Left unchecked, the danger is that years can go by before you get a chance to figure out whether your day-to-day life matches up with the things that are most important to you. It's important to ask yourself, on a fairly regular basis, whether your work and your relationships, home setup and routine, fit with your character. It's so important to develop an awareness of this. If your life and your work are out of kilter with your deepest values, you will feel dissatisfied. And when you feel dissatisfied, you'll be operating under par. If you're striving for goals that are pitched wrongly – you have your 'ladder propped up against the wrong wall' as the saying goes – it will impinge on your happiness and success in the long run. You're also more likely to end up feeling resentful and frustrated. Left unchecked, you may develop depression or anxiety as a result of the disconnect between your intrinsic values and your life.

In this chapter, you can find an exhaustive quiz to assess your character, delving into the deepest recesses of your personality and values. It will help you to identify who you are at a deep level and exactly what it is that matters to you.

When you're doing the quiz, it's incredibly important to keep the results private. Any answers are for your eyes only. In research, psychologists have found that when people know that someone else will read their answer in this type of questionnaire, they are less likely to answer personality assessments honestly.[12] And of course, if you aren't honest, the whole exercise is totally pointless. Some of the values that you hold most dear may seem totally unimportant to another person, and you may feel that there's a conflict between values and characteristics you *aspire* to identify with and those you are instinctively drawn to. This is perfectly natural, but you must resist the urge to allow this to inform your answers. Be totally honest. So, what if you think there are other traits or values that are more 'worthy' or indicative of success? They are not relevant if they don't matter to you.

---

12. Tests have shown that people tend to score consistently higher for positive personality traits when they are answering a personality test as part of a job application than they do when there is no specific reason for doing the test. We 'edit' ourselves when we think somebody else is watching.

Developing a keen awareness of your values gives you a sense of clarity that helps give you confidence in asserting yourself in all areas of your life. In my case, it has also given me the strength to call it out when I feel that my deep values are under attack.

I'll give you an example. One of the things at work that is most important to me is the language that people use to address one another. I find swearing extremely offensive and unnecessary. In my first job, out of university, this was a real issue. I was working for a hedge fund on Wall Street, and swearing was rife. What's more, it was the type of swearing that was generally accompanied with macho posturing, and was often directed at individuals as a way to blame and humiliate. When I complained about it, I was told I needed to take boxing lessons. The implication was that I should toughen up and keep my head down. It doesn't take a genius to see that this was a veiled form of misogyny. I was one of very few women in the business at a time when women were still expected to 'man up' in order to get on.

I left that job not long afterwards, and the aggressive, hyper-masculine culture (of which the sweary group-speak was an obvious symptom) was one of the main reasons I didn't want to stay. More recently, I have found that how people treat one another at work has become even more important to me. As I was climbing the ladder there were behaviours that I tolerated simply because they seemed part of the corporate world. But as I've got older and, hopefully, a little wiser, I no longer have patience with anyone who leads by fear. We all spend a huge amount of time at work and it's imperative it's a place of positive energy rather than a drain.

This is why I found Pitney Bowes, where I currently work, so refreshing – everyone was ready to help. Sure, things are not perfect, but they never are. Everyone is on board, working together to help the company transform.

For me, the way employees are treated in an organization is of paramount importance. The culture *is* the business. Where blame culture becomes endemic, it's a symptom of wider organizational dysfunction. I do advise my mentees when they see this and cannot change it, that it really is time to move on.

Values are something that shift as you move through life. Flexibility is absolutely key to me now as a working mother, but it's something I didn't think twice about in my 20s. For Carbon's Marine Aubin, respect is one value that has become increasingly important to her: 'It matters more to me now than ever. When I feel this value is compromised by a colleague's behaviour, I call it out right away.' Acknowledging these shifting values can be challenging – I have sometimes had a pang as I imagine my former self shaking her head at me from the sidelines. 'I'm still driven,' I want to tell her: 'It's just that I've learnt from experience that I need to allow a life outside work too.'

I'm so set on this value of flexibility that it almost prevented me from taking the job at Pitney. When I first discussed the role, I was told that I would have to work in St Denis, which is more than an hour's commute from where I live. I told Pitney I could only take the job if I could work from my home office most of the time, and only go to St Denis for a weekly and monthly meeting. After a negotiation, they agreed, but it's something it wouldn't have occurred to me to negotiate on had I not been so aware of my values and priorities. The tough part of this is that I had to be willing to walk away if my new employers had refused to accommodate my needs. Thankfully, they were open to persuasion.

When your workplace chimes with your values, it's a happy place to be. When I joined Pitney Bowes, I couldn't believe how nice everybody was. I had never worked in an organization where there was such a positive, supportive culture. It showed me how the corporate norm has evolved to become something unnecessarily harsh and competitive. But it doesn't need to be every woman for herself. Cultivating the types of networks I talk about in the Community chapter helps to forge bonds that act as an antidote to this, but the values of an organization need to flow from the top down, too. In fact, before I came to work at Pitney Bowes, Johnna Torsone, the EVP of HR, told me that she wanted to be my mentor. This incredible gesture gave me access to the network I needed to be successful in the role.

Once we grasp the appeal of work that fits with individual values, it's clear that for organizations, whatever their size, brand values have to stand for something. PR buzzwords aren't enough – companies need to embody the values that they say they uphold. Whether it's creativity, curiosity, innovation or disruption, senior managers must ensure that there's a culture of support underpinning every team that allows these values to flourish. To use a gardening metaphor, the soil needs to be rich to maximize growth. Success isn't all down to the quality of the seeds. The nurturing capability of the environment they are planted in makes the difference between plants that thrive and those that simply survive.

Read through the list below and write a letter next to each value: V = Very important, Q = Quite important, and N = Not so important; and make sure to score *at least ten* in each category. Aim to start off with as many as you can in the V category without stretching the truth.

☐ **Acceptance:** to be open to and accepting of myself, others, life, etc.

☐ **Adventure:** to be adventurous; to actively seek, create or explore novel or stimulating experiences

☐ **Assertiveness:** to respectfully stand up for my rights and request what I want

☐ **Authenticity:** to be authentic, genuine, real; to be true to myself

☐ **Beauty:** to appreciate, create, nurture or cultivate beauty in myself, others, the environment

☐ **Caring:** to be caring towards myself, others, the environment, etc.

☐ **Challenge:** to keep challenging myself to grow, learn, improve

☐ **Compassion:** to act with kindness towards those who are suffering

☐ **Connection:** to engage fully in whatever I am doing, and be fully present with others

☐ **Contribution:** to contribute, help, assist or make a positive difference to myself or others

☐ **Conformity:** to be respectful and obedient of rules and obligations

☐ **Cooperation:** to be cooperative and collaborative with others

☐ **Courage:** to be courageous or brave; to persist in the face of fear, threat or difficulty

☐ **Creativity:** to be creative or innovative

☐ **Curiosity:** to be curious, open-minded and interested; to explore and discover

☐ **Encouragement:** to encourage and reward behaviour that I value in myself or others

☐ **Equality:** to treat others as equal to myself, and vice versa

☐ **Excitement:** to seek, create and engage in activities that are exciting, stimulating or thrilling

☐ **Fairness:** to be fair to myself or others

☐ **Fitness:** to maintain or improve my fitness; to look after my physical and mental health and wellbeing

☐ **Flexibility:** to adjust and adapt readily to changing circumstances

☐ **Financial stability/Independence:** to support myself financially

☐ **Freedom:** to live freely; to choose how I live and behave, or help others do likewise

☐ **Friendliness:** to be friendly, companionable, or agreeable towards others

☐ **Forgiveness:** to be forgiving towards myself or others

☐ **Fun:** to be fun-loving; to seek, create, and engage in fun-filled activities

☐ **Generosity:** to be generous, sharing and giving, to myself or others

☐ **Gratitude:** to be grateful for and appreciative of the positive aspects of myself, others and life

☐ **Honesty:** to be honest, truthful and sincere with myself and others

☐ **Humour:** to see and appreciate the humorous side of life

☐ **Humility:** to be humble or modest; to let my achievements speak for themselves

☐ **Industry:** to be industrious, hard-working, dedicated

☐ **Independence:** to be self-supportive and choose my own way of doing things

☐ **Intimacy:** to open up, reveal, and share myself – emotionally or physically – in my close personal relationships

☐ **Justice:** to uphold justice and fairness

☐ **Kindness:** to be kind, compassionate, considerate, nurturing or caring towards myself or others

☐ **Love:** to act lovingly or affectionately towards myself or others

☐ **Mindfulness:** to be conscious of, open to, and curious about my here-and-now experience

☐ **Order:** to be orderly and organized

☐ **Open-mindedness:** to think things through, see things from others' points of view and weigh evidence fairly

☐ **Patience:** to wait calmly for what I want

☐ **Persistence:** to continue resolutely, despite problems or difficulties

☐ **Pleasure:** to create and give pleasure to myself or others

☐ **Power:** to strongly influence or wield authority over others, e.g. taking charge, leading, organizing

☐ **Reciprocity:** to build relationships in which there is a fair balance of giving and taking

☐ **Respect:** to be respectful towards myself or others; to be polite, considerate and show positive regard

☐ **Responsibility:** to be responsible and accountable for my actions

☐ **Romance:** to be romantic; to display and express love or strong affection

☐ **Safety:** to secure, protect or ensure safety of myself or others

☐ **Self-awareness:** to be aware of my own thoughts, feelings and actions

☐ **Self-care:** to look after my health and wellbeing and get my needs met

☐ **Self-development:** to keep growing, advancing or improving in knowledge, skills, character or life experience

☐ **Self-control:** to act in accordance with my own ideals

☐ **Sensuality:** to create, explore and enjoy experiences that stimulate the five senses

☐ **Sexuality:** to explore or express my sexuality

☐ **Spirituality:** to connect with things bigger than myself

☐ **Skilfulness:** to continually practise and improve my skills, and apply myself fully when using them

☐ **Status:** to feel successful and significant in comparison to others

☐ **Supportiveness:** to be supportive, helpful, encouraging and available to myself or others

☐ **Trust:** to be trustworthy; to be loyal, faithful, sincere and reliable

Insert your own unlisted values here:

You should end up with at least ten values on your 'Very Important' list. Together, the 'Very/Quite Important' columns should have 40 values listed.

Now you need to whittle it down further. Take your time to identify the ones that are really important to you. Don't try to do this in one sitting. Cut your list down over a period of days until you have four values left in each of your categories. It may be that the answers surprise you. It may also become clear that your job, lifestyle or current situation is at odds with your core values. If this is the case, it's time to set about creating a life that fits them better. This might mean radical changes to your career, your relationships, even the fundamentals of everyday life, from where you live to who you spend your time with.

Having a confident grasp of your core values will give you clarity of purpose: a sense that your life has meaning. This will improve your overall wellbeing. In studies, attempts to chase happiness have been shown to correlate with a negative impact on mood, whereas those who focus more on striving towards a sense of meaning and purpose report greater overall satisfaction with their lives. In a paper published last year in the *Review of General Psychology* in the US, Cornell psychologists Login George and Crystal Park identified three key features of 'purpose' – the degree to which individuals feel directed and motivated by their valued life goals; their ability to comprehend and make sense out of their experiences and view them as part of a coherent whole; and a feeling of significance and value in the world.[13]

Taking the time to explore your character and to identify the values that matter to you is an important first step towards developing your sense of purpose. Like confidence and clarity, it is another long-term project, something to be fine-tuned, worked at and revisited regularly.

Generally speaking, female values tend to tip more in the direction of empathy and context-informed judgements whilst men are more likely to be self-focused and have rigid moral codes and rules that they apply whatever the nuances of a situation. This is a sweeping statement, but it's one with pretty sound research behind it, so I think it's worth paying it some attention.[14] Many studies show that women are more empathetic than men. When men and women watch wrongdoers being punished, men show activation in the reward centre of their brain, whereas women's brains show activation in their pain zone, indicating empathy for suffering even when it is perceived to be justly deserved.

Women have also been found to be more likely to factor personal cost into decisions about whether to punish a stranger. Women tend to be more generous when asked to share with a stranger, and they are more likely to reciprocate acts of kindness. It is hard to argue that these common feminine traits, including empathy, egalitarianism and judgements that pay

---

13. www.psycnet.apa.org/journals/gpr/20/3/205/

14. www.psychologytoday.com/blog/experiments-in-philosophy/201005/sex-the-bench-do-women-and-men-have-different-moral-values

heed to context as well as principle, are anything but a force for good in the workplace.

Traditionally, typically male character traits have been thought of as the prerequisites for leadership. Dominance, charisma, aggression. But increasingly, more feminine traits are coming to the fore. Gillian Jones, an executive coach who is the founder of Emerge UK development consultancy, has created many women's empowerment programmes. It's her belief that focusing on our own talents, rather than trying to emulate the ones you think you need to appear strong or dominant, is key to success: 'Women often have a high level of emotional intelligence and if they trust their intuition they will probably be great influencers. Building on these strengths is far more important than trying to emulate macho behaviour.'

In order for these traits to become more widely accepted as the leadership strengths they are, we need the corporate world to shift its mindset. At the moment, so often, these traits are written off as unhelpful. You may be told you're 'too emotional', 'too personally invested', 'too maternal', 'too detail-focused'. I've been called all of these things, and it drives me crazy because whilst there can be some downsides to these attributes, there are also huge commercial and strategic upsides too.

The 'mothering' criticism is the most infuriating of all. I was criticized for this when I was charged with making some redundancies in my team years ago when the company was being restructured. I helped one of them to negotiate a better retirement package than she'd been expecting and helped facilitate a departmental move for another. I treated my staff as people rather than numbers. I saw the personal consequences of the decisions that the company had made on their behalf. This, to the minds of my managers, was an indication that I was 'too attached' to them.

I argued that the staff member who made the transfer was an asset who went on to have a great career in a different area of the business, and that the woman who took retirement did so feeling positive about her long career at the company. She had a broad and influential network where any indirect negative fallout could have had a wide-reaching negative impact on the image of the business.

Similarly, when women are criticized for being 'overly focused on the detail', there is sometimes a valid point – in order to progress to more senior positions in a business, it's important to be able to step back and see the bigger picture. But a passion for detail can be invaluable, too. Asking extra questions and delving a little deeper into the minutiae of a situation or proposition can provide important due diligence. Likewise, questioning the grounding for big-picture decisions, and interrogating the foundations of any assumptions an organization is taking for granted, can save time and resources in the long run (although it doesn't always make you popular).

An incisive picture of the traits that make for a strong leader comes via the late self-help pioneer Napoleon Hill. He was an American journalist interested in success, and he studied the lives of over 25,000 high achievers to find out what they had in common. He shadowed some of the greatest lead-ers of his generation, from Andrew Carneige to Henry Ford. Here are the 11 traits he said were key to them all:

1. Unwavering Courage
Full belief in oneself and one's occupation.

2. Self-Control
You can't control others unless you control yourself.

3. A Keen Sense of Justice
Essential for maintaining respect of your followers.

4. Definiteness of Decision
Nobody likes to follow a leader who is unsure.

5. Definiteness of Plans
Having a plan and sticking to it.

6. The Habit of Doing More Than Paid For
All leaders who succeed are always willing to do more than they require from their followers.

7. A Pleasing Personality
This is essential to ensure the respect of followers (whether these be customers, workers or shareholders).

8) Sympathy and Understanding
A successful leader understands their followers' problems.

9. Mastery of Detail
All great leaders have a keen eye for detail.

10. Willingness to Assume Full Responsibility
A successful leader must be willing to be responsible for the mistakes and shortcomings of their followers.

11. Cooperation
As well as cooperating with others, a successful leader must also induce his/her followers to cooperate. Leadership calls for power and power requires cooperation.

When working with women who doubt their leadership abilities I often use this list to demonstrate that women often inately have the natural charater traits that would make them great leaders.

CLARITY

*'Seeking clarity is seeking connection with
the universe. To connect is to understand;
to be clear is to be enlightened.'*
Annie Zalezsak

ONCE YOU'VE ACCEPTED THAT every step of your career,
you are shaping your future through the power of your
choices, it's important to ensure that you develop a disci-
pline of focus. You need clarity on the things that matter
to you so that you can identify your priorities. Once you
have this, you'll be far less likely to get distracted by other
people's needs.

Our associations with the concept of clarity are themselves unhelpful and misleading. We think of it as an organic
thing, something that occurs after a period of reflection and
exploration, in moments of epiphany and inspiration. But
clarity is something you have to work at. Rather than waiting for clarity to emerge, you need to summon it proactively.
Clarity grows from focused effort. Developing a process to
help strengthen your own sense of clarity is a worthwhile
investment in your future.

SAY IT LOUD, GET IT DONE

Each year, I encourage all my staff to decide what they want to concentrate on for the next 12 months. These should be five to seven concrete aims that cover all areas of your life: work, health, home, relationships. Half of these aims should be personal, half work related. I recommend spending an hour or two really thinking deeply about these and noting down your thoughts. How do you want your life to grow in the year ahead?

When you're identifying your aims, make sure they aren't so general that you're unsure what they mean ('Move career forward', for example). Likewise, ensure that they aren't too narrow either ('Join a running club and go once a week').

I'll give you an example of some of my own:

'I want more quality time with my children, where I engage with them fully.'

'I want to speak and write publicly about women and the workplace.'

'I want to delight my clients and my employees with the service I provide.'

'I want to have time for deep, strategic thinking at work.'

'I want to feel good in my own skin.'

'I want to feel calm and in control.'

You might think, reading these, that this is an exercise that tells you what you already know. But it's quite the opposite. The power of this simple assignment is remarkable. This is because most of us are out of touch with our own deep-held hopes and desires. We tell ourselves there's no time for them, that the business of grown-up life trumps them.

This simple exercise can have profound and far-reaching consequences. Especially if you share the outcome with friends and family. Writing something down is the expression of an intention. As soon as I made writing one of my official areas of focus, I started to prioritize it. I'd been thinking about it, vaguely, for the past 15 years and people often told me I should write a book, but it wasn't until I made a clear intention that I took action on it. Once you've committed to something in this way, your subconscious kicks in and directs your energies to make it happen.

I recently found some old notebooks from my late teens and early 20s. I was in the habit of writing down my bucket lists: 'Before I'm 30' and 'Before I'm 40'. These books had been gathering dust for years by the time I stumbled on them again. But what was remarkable, opening them, was how many of my goals I had actually achieved. I had even written down 'live in Paris', which I found myself doing, almost by accident, it seemed, when we moved there for my husband's job 19 years ago. Likewise, I'd written down 'have my first child' as a goal to achieve before I was 30, and I smiled when I read this again. I had Qaahir when I was 29.

So why is it that it requires an exercise of this type to get in touch with our true wants? It's partly because women are primed to tune in to other people's needs and forget their own. When there's a surfeit of 'noise' in your life and you're surrounded by other people's demands and requests, your own priorities can get so pushed to the back of the queue that they get buried. With countless other voices shouting their demands over the top of your own (many of these being urgent), your needs get missed.

The long-term result is deep dissatisfaction and resentment. If you continue to live in this way, you'll find yourself looking back over the past year (or the past five years) thinking, 'Where did that time *go*?'. Of course, nobody wants to be in that position.

In contrast, once you've identified your areas of focus, you can start taking action. Make sure they relate to your whole life, not just to work. It's really important to include a goal that relates to health and wellbeing as this underpins your capacity to function optimally in every other area of your life.

Share your aims with your friends and family. The more you speak about them, the more 'real' they become to you. I'm going to talk in more detail about scheduling your time to align with your goals later in this chapter.

Sometimes it takes a major renegotiation of your work practices in order to achieve this. This may be tough and require some serious discussion at work and potentially at home too. When I was promoted to European DMT sales at Pitney, I quickly realized that the precedent (back-to-back meetings) made my goal of spending three full days out of the office with clients an impossibility. My diary was packed. When I wasn't expected at a meeting, I was booked on a call. The expectation of senior management was that I would keep up with all of these scheduled appointments.

In part, it's work practices like this (along with a precedent of doing the job as it has been done in a certain way in the past) that stops many women from applying for senior jobs in the first place. It's easy to assume there's no room for rethinking, for building in more flexibility, for changing the routine. That the routine *is* the job. But just because something has been done in one way in the past doesn't mean that it's the best, or only way, that role can work. A good employer will be open to renegotiation on processes and procedure, particularly if it leads to efficiency and cost savings in the long run.

My job was to manage the European sales team. In the past, this had been done by weekly individual calls with each of the countries I was responsible for – up to 22 sellers. I would then have to take my notes from the call and summarize them for three different groups of people. This took a lot of time. With the advantage of a newcomer's perspective, I could see that this was a huge waste of effort.

There was an online CRM system designed for these sellers to input all the information discussed in these calls. If it was used as intended, it would provide a live at-a-glance snapshot of all the sales managers – where they were on negotiations with individual clients, how they were doing with their targets and whether there was anything to flag up. But it wasn't being used consistently by staff. I proposed dropping the calls with individual sellers and encouraging them to update the system regularly instead. I chased up the ones who didn't do what I'd asked, but within a couple of weeks, it was running smoothly and there was no need for the calls.

My direct reports now had more autonomy and could get on with their jobs. All the sellers responded well to the new regime – they had all been frustrated with the unnecessary calls. I firmly believe that in the vast majority of cases, competent staff thrive best in an environment where they are given the agency and flexibility to get things done in the way they think best, without being micromanaged.

Managing upwards was trickier. I was supposed to have a weekly call with my European consolidator on a Wednesday. This would sometimes take two to three hours. On Thursday, I'd have a call with the global sales/product team. But the problem was that these two calls meant I needed to be in the office for those two days. With my target to spend three full days out of the office with clients, I knew I needed to rethink these calls and find a more time-efficient way of checking in. I didn't change anything when I started – I let the first quarter of the year go by so that I could gauge how well the processes were working.

I suggested a reduction in the lengths of my formal weekly calls with my managers and we implemented this. The benefits were immediately obvious. We stuck more to an agenda and didn't get distracted. Outside of these calls, I still spoke to my managers a lot, but the reduction of the formal calls made a big difference.

Although it took a bit of persuasion, opposition to the new changes didn't always come from the top down. This has been the case in my most recent job too. When I started in November, there was a precedent of Monday, Wednesday, Thursday and Friday calls with the sales team. Many of the same people (18 out of 20) were on all of these calls – there was a lot of overlap – clearly a crazy waste of resources. Often, we were saying more or less the same thing on these calls.

When I suggested cutting them to Wednesday and Friday, the resistance to this came foremost from the individual staff who attached importance to the calls, particularly those who led the calls. But they quickly felt the benefit in terms of their own time. Likewise, as soon as senior staff began to see the evidence that my client-focused strategy was working, they dropped any opposition they may have felt initially to my changes. In fact, my direct manager, Jason Dies, President of DMT Pitney Bowes states: 'I love working with Shemin because she's so efficient – she cuts out everything unnecessary from my calendar.'

This is a good example of a time when I was able to follow my instinct, go against the grain and get it right. But I had to stay mindful of my colleagues' concerns when implementing the new structure, and ensure I communicated the reasons for my changes with clarity. As a result, I was able to get everybody on board despite their initial reservations.

SCHEDULING: THE KEY TO CLARITY

Planning your time is so important if you want to stick to a clear set of goals and objectives. You need to be possessive about your own time, to guard it fiercely. One of the best ways to do this is to draw up a weekly schedule and apportion blocks of time to the activities you want to focus on. These can be specific work tasks, thinking time, visits to clients and personal appointments. If you have an online diary, particularly if it's one that colleagues, managers or secretarial staff access, ensure that you block out these times in your diary.

Peter Bregman's book *18 Minutes: Find Your Focus, Master Distraction and Get the Right Things Done*, offers lots of inspiring ways to rethink the way you prioritize. Too often, he says, a to-do list becomes an 'I'm-never-going-to-get-to-it' list. He describes it as: 'An inventory of everything we want to do, plan to do, think we should do…' going on to argue that: 'The problem with typical to-do lists is that we use them as our primary tool to guide our daily accomplishments. But it's the wrong tool. A to-do list is a useful collection tool – it's there to help us make sure we know the pool of things we need to get done.'

In their book *ReWork*, David Heinemeier Hanson and Jason Fried are similarly sceptical about the helpfulness of traditional to-do lists: 'Long lists are guilt trips. Break all of them down into a bunch of smaller lists, that way, when you've completed an item on a list, you've ticked off 10% of the tasks, rather than 1%. You still have the same amount of stuff left to do but now you can look at the small picture and find satisfaction, motivation and progress. A lot better than staring at the huge picture and feeling demoralized.'

On top of this, Bregman argues we need to identify the areas of priority that are important to us for the year ahead, then when we're planning each day, divide the day into the same six categories. Tasks then get filed in one of these areas. His recommendation that only 5% of time should be spent on tasks that fall outside these areas seems unrealistic to me, so I've adapted mine to 15% of time. His daily to-do lists look like the one overleaf (filled in with an example from my own week):

To delight my clients and staff with the service and management I deliver.

- To promote organically to encourage career progression of my team.
- To create financial structures that allow clients to purchase in a manner that fits with their budgets.

To write and speak about women in business.

- To publish this book!
- To work on my TEDx talk.

To have time for deep strategic thinking.

- To make time for breakthrough thinking for my business.
- To create unusual but effective partnerships for the business.

Have more quality time with my kids where I am focused and connected.

- Have dinner with my children every evening, and make it a tech-free zone.
- To ensure I don't miss any parent/teacher evenings or performances.
- To do one fun thing a month with each child.

To feel good in my own skin, calm and in control.

- To work out three to five times a week.
- To visit the doctor regularly.
- To breathe correctly and meditate for five minutes per day.

THE OTHER 15%[15]

- To keep on top of grocery shopping.
- To keep on top of personal admin.

---

15. Bregman suggests 5%.

Creating a daily to-do table along these lines is a great way to align your daily tasks with your goals. And it's a brilliant way to tackle overwhelm that can lead to paralysis. It really can help you to overcome that feeling when the ridiculous and ever-increasing barrage of things 'to do' right now makes you want to run for the hills.

When you have too much to do, living in the moment can have its drawbacks. For all its fashionable mindful benefits, as Bregman says: 'Sometimes, focusing on the present is the obstacle. For example, if you didn't look ahead to see where the road was going when you are driving, you'd keep driving straight and crash at the next curve.'

A smart table such as the one above is a great way to ensure your itinerary for the day is aligned with your own bigger picture. It also enables you to see, immediately, anything that doesn't fit with your goals. You can either choose to accommodate such tasks in the spare 15% of time allotted, or turn your back on them. It's so important to be clear enough about your priorities that you have the confidence to walk away from opportunities or requests that aren't going to help you advance.

Another good analogy for this checking mechanism is open-water swimming. In a race, you need to swim consistently and quickly. But when you're face down in a large expanse of water, you have no way of knowing whether you're moving in the right direction. It's all too easy to power on, without checking, and before you know it, you've struck out off-course and find yourself far away from the pack, perhaps even further away from the finish line than you were when you started. You need to keep looking up at the horizon: 'sighting' as it's called. You only need to do this for a split second, but you need to do it regularly, to ensure that you're staying on course.

Spending a few minutes at the beginning of every day or at the end of the previous day to make sure that your task list fits with your broader goals is equivalent to this. This 'sighting' for the day will help to propel you in the direction you intend to go. And checking in regularly will ensure you keep your shifting priorities in mind. Once you extrapolate the benefit of this over a period of weeks or months, it's a great tool to help you stick to your goals and avoid getting blown off course, however tempting the outside influences that might spring up in your path.

'When I was young in my career I would stay in the office until midnight or later, enjoying the time with my co-workers and believing I was putting in the extra effort to get me ahead,' says one senior IBM staffer we talked to. 'I was also free of any thoughts of being seen to be less than committed. After family and children forced me to prioritize my time, I realized more and more that it is results that matter, not hours. We should all be measured and rewarded based on our results. I leave to go home for my son and as a manager this means I don't drive meetings late in the day unless it's critical. I aim to empower my team to choose their own working and life priorities.'

STOP PEOPLE PLEASING

When you accommodate other people's demands repeatedly, you're sending a message that you'll always accept last-minute requests and put your own needs last. You're telling the world that you're happy to pick up the slack, bend over backwards to squeeze your priorities (even when it's your day job) in wherever you can. That you're happy to give away your time to make other people's lives easier. Ask yourself whether this is the message you want to give.

If it isn't, creating a daily table such as the one on page 72 is a great way to adopt a more realistic approach to your time. You can use it to block your daily workload into your diary. Any major tasks should be written in, whether that's a report, research or a proposal. If you don't note these down, you run the risk of other people filling your diary up with meetings and requests, which means you have to fit your actual work into time that should be your own. The net result? Endless overtime.

And here's another powerful tip from *ReWork* to help you manage your workload: 'Avoid saying "this is high priority, this is low priority." Or: "this is a 1, this is a 2, this is a 3…." You'll just end up with a long list of high priority items. Instead, prioritize visually, put the most important thing on top and start with that.'

Ideally, those tasks that tie in with your most significant life goals should always be sitting at the top of this list. If they aren't, it's a sign you're probably in the wrong job.

SETTING CLEAR BOUNDARIES: THE ART OF SAYING 'NO'

For many women, cultivating an appearance of willingness may seem an obvious way to win favour at work. It makes you seem agreeable, you might think, someone to be relied upon. But the problem is that it can quickly get you labelled as an office doormat. Being upfront about the amount of time you need to do your job well and asserting yourself by physically writing your tasks into your diary demonstrates organization, confidence and foresight. Colleagues may baulk at first but they'll soon get used to it.

Carbon's Marine Aubin again: 'For many years I took on anything my bosses threw at me. I said yes constantly, and prided myself on the speed and quality of my work. But the result was that I'd had three burn-outs by the time I was 27. It was unsustainable and I had to face up to the fact I wasn't a machine.'

Since I met Marine, last year, I have seen her shift to a position where she's comfortable with saying 'No', with assertiveness and confidence. She says: 'Despite my misgivings, I quickly realized that clients and colleagues responded really well when I set more boundaries. By demonstrating that I respect myself and my time, I have found that other people are more likely to reflect that back to me. People like it when other people display clarity and self-respect. I always felt this way myself about other people, but it came as a revelation to discover that I could apply it to myself and benefit from it. I finally feel in charge of my time. It's as if a huge weight has been lifted from me.'

Marine had to practise saying no: 'I started by passing on small stuff: work drinks when I had personal plans; a request for help from a junior team member when I knew there was somebody else who could assist them. It felt strange, but I got more confident the more I did it. And it got me to a position where I was able to push back on bigger demands: an extra project I didn't have the capacity for; a conference or an interview that someone else could do. I started asking myself: "For the time I'm going to spend on this, is it worth it for me?" I couldn't believe I had never questioned other people's demands in this way before.'

Marine says she also adjusted her management style. 'I made sure I communicated more clearly. I became more hands-off. I set a deadline, discussed it with the team member I'd assigned it to, then left them to it. I made it clear I expected it to be done by the deadline unless I was warned in advance about a delay.'

When I decided to take charge of my own time at work, I began to read a lot of self-help books, and listened to endless TED talks by motivational speakers. I wanted to gather wisdom from wherever I could, to learn how to be more efficient and clear about the way I used my time. Some of this advice was invaluable – but it wasn't the long-term solution I hoped it would be to help create more time. For me, as for many women, the more efficient I was, the more work I was given, the more favours were asked of me, the more I felt obligated to say 'yes' to extra requests. I ended up doing more, and I hadn't gained the extra time I needed for deep thinking and strategy.

Now, I've got smarter at managing my time and my deadlines. As a result, I get much more meaningful work done. For instance, even if I'm done with a task two days before the deadline, I won't send it before the morning of the deadline (except if it can help a whole project moving forward much quicker of course). This way, I avoid having bosses and clients throwing more tasks at me with low added value. The sorts of things that other people just don't want to do, but could. If I have free time and all the tasks for my other goals are done, I also prefer to offer to work on something specific that's interesting – challenging in career and personal development terms.

When I was preparing my TEDx talk, I looked for inspiration from those who had gone before me. One that really resonated with me as it gave lots of insight into this topic was Adam Grant's TED Talk: 'Are you a giver or a taker?'. It's heartening to anyone who has giving tendencies as he explores research that shows that the best performers at work are more likely to be givers than takers. Of course, there's a balance to be struck, and it's a tricky one to get right. Grant references Adam Rifkin, who observes a giving practice he calls the 'five-minute favour' – doing micro deeds for other people, from writing a LinkedIn reference to introducing two of your contacts. These are gestures that require minimal effort (and time) on your part, but give you a feel-good payoff and create an impression of generosity. A smarter move, perhaps, than saying yes to extra hours of overtime you won't get the credit for. With five-minute favours, it's perfectly possible to be a giver without becoming a martyr.

Guarding against being over-generous with your time makes strategic sense. It'll free your headspace up for big picture thinking. So, if you feel you could do a better job by saying 'No' to more requests, the onus is on you to make this explicit. You owe it to yourself at least to ask.

As Grant says, 'Adam Rifkin taught me that giving doesn't require becoming Mother Teresa or Mahatma Gandhi; we can all find ways of adding high value to others' lives at a low personal cost. The five-minute favor is my single favorite habit that I learnt while writing my book.'

MAKING TIME TO THINK

I'm going to share a story with you that illustrates the importance of prioritizing thinking time, and how I came to realize that this is key to developing the mental clarity that's necessary if you want to do a strategic job well.

When I started at IBM, I was invited to the next gen training conference to hear the Chief Executive, Lou Gerstner, speak. In the canteen on the first day of the course, I went to the gym and I grabbed some breakfast. Rather than sitting with my colleagues, I looked around the canteen and noticed an older man on his own at a table, so I sat down next to him and introduced myself.

I asked him what he did and he was vague, but told me he had been at IBM for less than a decade. I asked him about his biggest challenges. He told me that when he joined the company, there was an expectation that he'd be in back-to-back meetings. He had no time to think. He told me that every day he asked his secretary to block out at least an hour or two for reflection. This was the only way he would have the space required to think of solutions.

I had to cut our conversation short to dash off before the big presentation. I remember thinking, 'He may be a senior staffer, but he clearly has time on his hands. I could never carve out that kind of time with my workload…' But (you've probably seen this coming) I was shocked and embarrassed when the very same man walked on to the stage to present. He was the Chief Executive himself!

It was a memorable day, and what he said really stayed with me. When you're consumed by doing, you lose perspective. You need to build pauses into your week in order to give your mind the space to think. Even if it feels like luxury rather than necessity, a few weeks of sticking to these enforced thinking breaks will reap rewards and convince you of their value. If you don't plan these 'blue sky' windows, expecting them to occur of their own accord, whilst you're frantically hopscotching from task to meeting to email, you're setting yourself up to fail.

Truly innovative thinking can only occur when you've had time to decompress. Richard Branson once said he has his best ideas in the shower, and countless other Chief Executives swear by a morning run or meditation as a great way to free up creative and strategic thought.

I have started to formally carve out space for deep thought in my schedule. In my current job, I block off 30–60-minute slots a few times a week to make sure I have space for this. It just shows as blocked time in my online calendar, so nobody questions it. I use it to work on long-term projects for our global team that I'd otherwise end up picking up after the work day when I was exhausted. Sometimes I use the time to grab a coffee with a colleague who is working on a project I want to get a more in-depth understanding of. Sometimes I go for a walk and a think. More often than not these tend to be the times of my 'aha!' moments.

SETTING A CLEAR PLAN FOR THE FUTURE

It may sound strange, but one of the first things I do when I start in any new job is to identify the person who I want to replace me when I leave. I start planning for progress immediately. It isn't just about legacy planning. In any senior job, the key to doing it well lies in successful delegation. Also, I understand that if I need to be able to take a real vacation (which I do), it's crucial that the staff who are left holding the fort are competent, capable and confident.

As a general rule, giving up detail is difficult. Nobody likes to be called out. But if you don't let go of some of the small stuff, you can't free yourself up to progress. It may feel uncomfortable to entrust the detail to your more junior staff, but it's an absolute necessity. This is something I learnt during my time in finance. Initially, in my CFO roles, I would try to hang on to the detail, staying at work later and later to keep on top of it.

One thing that helped me was shadowing Laurence Haziot, one of the general managers at IBM. I followed her for a day and saw how she delegated. She took notes constantly, and tried never to touch the same thing twice. For example, if she got an email, she read it, either deleted, filed or forwarded it and that was it. If she had to take action on it, she wrote it into her diary immediately, booking a time-slot for the task, whatever it was. In fact, I was so impressed with her that I became the CFO for her division.

I also got comfortable with the idea of failure. In the words of Ginni Romety, 'Fail fast and move on.' This builds on the advice I was given by my first ever manager, Dave

Kaja, who told me: 'It's fine to make mistakes, just don't make the same mistake twice.' Taking calculated risks is a necessity in any career. If you want to advance, you have to get comfortable with it.

Sometimes, it feels risky to delegate, but if you don't, you'll end up spending a lot of time on routine tasks that could easily be outsourced. This can lead to a situation where you're too swamped to do the less obvious networking, strategizing and empire building that opens doors to bigger things. It can be tough if your team includes experienced staffers, particularly older men, who may be unaccustomed to being managed by a woman and may feel uncomfortable about a new manager changing the way things are done, but delegating well really is a powerful key to success.

Having said that, it's extremely important for managers to factor in the workload of junior staffers when you're delegating: there's a difference between delegating and dumping on. Speaking as someone at the start of her career, Carbon's Georgina Hill says: 'Junior staffers have nobody to delegate to, so maintaining personal clarity and setting boundaries is harder for us. Confidence and assertiveness are key to this, and the ability to say "No" when we feel overburdened.

Whatever stage your career is at, and whether you have managerial responsibilities or not, Sheryl Sandberg's advice is helpful: 'Counterintuitively, long-term success at work often depends on not trying to meet every demand placed on us.'[16]

---

16. Sheryl Sandberg, *Lean In* (WH Allen, 2015)

Gillian Jones, author and founder of Emerge UK, a development consultancy who specialize in executive training, agrees. 'I still have many clients who request my services specifically and I always find it difficult to say no to them, therefore I've spent more time and effort in the business rather than on the business. I probably could have grown my company faster if I had been more willing to delegate more work out and be more strategic with my business. It's something I'm still working on.'

For Jones, as for all of us, maintaining a clear vision for your future and sticking to it is a process: something we need to keep revising and reminding ourselves of. Planning for the future should be approached with a flexible attitude and an acceptance that life goals need to be thought about in a long-term way. For example, flexible working and shorter hours may be right for now, but that doesn't mean it's forever. Clarity doesn't have to equal rigidity.

CONSISTENCY

*'We become what we want to be by consistently
being what we want to become each day.'*
Richard G. Scott

WHETHER IN PUBLIC LIFE, parenting or personal relationships, one of the most underrated behaviours is
consistency. Because of its unsexiness, it often gets forgotten.
Chipping away at a task, whether it's a discreet project or a
huge life goal, somehow seems less exciting than great feats
of endurance or bursts of productivity. When it comes to
work, it's easy to fall into an all or nothing approach: alter-
nating productive spells with intervals of relative apathy.
Some of us may be more suited to this oscillation than
others – if you are the type of person who crammed like
crazy for 24 hours before an exam, then you're more likely
to fall into this camp in your working life.

Instead, sticking to a set routine and working within a
habitual framework is more likely to deliver results in the
long term. Research shows conscientiousness (consistency's
little sister) is more of a predictor of success than extrover-
sion or academic achievement, yet it isn't as often celebrated

by parents, teachers and employers.[17] In studies, people who score high on conscientiousness are more likely to earn more and report greater job satisfaction.[18] It impacts on everything from productivity to likeability, wealth to health. It even positively correlates with the ability to sustain a marriage. Psychologist Brent Roberts of the University of Illinois studies conscientiousness and defines it as being linked to 'hygiene' factors such as organizational ability and forethought. 'Most people become more consistent with age,' he says. Although these behaviours come more naturally to people who are intrinsically conscientious, we can all learn from them.

In the same way that I think of confidence as something that needs to be practised, conscientiousness can also be self-taught. And the more you apply yourself with consistency, the more conscientious you become.

GOOD FOR BUSINESS

The appeal of consistency is obvious when you start to think about it. It's one thing having a friend who is inconsistent: sometimes great company but prone to cancel at the last minute, or throw out insensitive comments on a bad day. But in a work context, people are the public face of any business – ambassadors for the brand. As such, there is no room for contrary or hot-cold behaviour. If you're in a client-facing role, or a high-profile internal position, your

17. www.link.springer.com/article/10.1007/s10212-011-0099-9

18. www.ncbi.nlm.nih.gov/pmc/articles/PMC2747784

line manager will want to feel sure they can rely on you to behave in a way that they expect. Likewise, if you're in a more supportive role, colleagues will rely on you – they need you to do your job so they can do theirs. Delivering on this, presenting a conscientious front by demonstrating consistent behaviour over time, is a great way to build a strong personal brand.

For anyone struggling to make promotion and ascend the corporate hierarchy, and for women who are launching businesses and winning new clients, consistency and conscientiousness are great traits to embody. Creating an impression of consistency will help establish your reputation, ensuring clients and colleagues know what to expect from you. Setting clear expectations and delivering on them is the ultimate sales pitch – for you and your company.

CONSISTENCY AND AUTHENTICITY

We are all drawn to people who are consistent. Consistency is a mark of authenticity. There's an unease that creeps in when you don't feel you know where you stand with someone, or can't get a handle on who they are. Consistent people are more likely to be described as 'straight down the line', 'reliable' and 'a safe pair of hands'. People trust those who have a track record of success – but it's impossible to establish a consistent track record if you keep changing tack. They also tend to be the managers that employees follow when they move!

Behavioural psychology tells us that what you do has much more power than what you say. It's as true in parenting and interpersonal relationships as it is in the office. Consistent behaviour builds trust. Particularly if you're in a leadership position, you're showing your staff that you mean what you say, which will give them far more faith in any incentives and praise you may offer them in the future. Gandhi's famous phrase puts it best: 'Be the change you wish to see.' It's a great rule of thumb for anyone wanting to set a consistent example in the way that they behave and interact with others in the workplace.

Consistency brings results outside of work too. A consistent approach is the best way to instigate lasting change, whether in a relationship or your health. I'm going to share a personal example with you. My weight has fluctuated since my teens. Until recently, I'd always had a stop-start approach to exercise. I'd sign up for the gym in January, and go religiously for the first month, then stop. I'd take up jogging, then find that other things got in the way. It was the same with dieting.

It was demoralizing and it got me down in a low-level way every day. I resigned myself to accepting that my body was something I was likely to battle with forever. But I wasn't happy in my skin and I wanted to do something about it.

My husband, in contrast, runs every day, rain or shine, for 45 minutes. He has done this since we met in our early 20s. I envy him the single-mindedness he has adopted when it comes to his fitness, and over the years I've told myself it is a typically male trait: this ability to prioritize one's own needs come what may. The truth is, however, it's sometimes a question of willpower too and the consistent practice of the behaviour.

CONSISTENT HABIT-MAKING... AND BREAKING

It's catch-22. The more momentum you build up, doing something repeatedly until it becomes habitual, the more the behaviour becomes ingrained and as a result, the stronger your resolve to stick with it. You're less likely to quit. But if you don't stick at it long enough to build that momentum, you can't get started.

Most of us don't realize how many habits we have until we try to break them. It's hard, whether it's quitting Diet Coke (something I found almost impossible after years of addiction), or something more serious. Habits are hardwired into your brain, so un-learning them is hard. It's important to replace an unhealthy old habit with a healthy new one. In the case of my Coke habit, I switched to water with lemon or the real thing as a treat.

In his book on super-companies, Jim C. Collins the author of *Good to Great* tells the story of the first successful expedition to the South Pole. This has become a famous tortoise-and-hare-style allegory. It's often retold as it teaches us so much about the value of consistency.

THE TORTOISE WINS

Roald Amundsen's team beat Scott's to the South Pole by 34 days. Captain Scott's team famously died on their return journey, a consequence of a stop-start strategy that went wrong. Their varied pace approach (striking out for long stretches on days when the weather was favourable, and hunkering down when it wasn't) turned out to be far riskier than a consistent approach. As a result, they ran out of food and grew weak. In contrast, Amundsen's team's approach was steady. They kept a constant pace, sticking to a target of 20 miles per day, whatever the conditions.

At first glance, Scott's approach looks sensible: there's something almost primevally captivating about a feast-or-famine approach to tackling any major life goal. Conserving energy, then going flat out when the conditions are right. But this is risky, and the danger is that the weather is unpredictable. It's more prudent to keep pushing on regardless.

Whether it's writing a book, mastering a skill such as playing a musical instrument, or introducing a lifestyle habit such as meditating, doing it little and often and keeping at it consistently, really works in the long term.

This approach also happens to be a great antidote to procrastination. When you aren't waiting for the conditions to be right – whether that's your energy level, 'inspiration' striking you, or worrying about whether you've got the motivation to go flat out on a given day, you just get on and do it. Circumstances don't need to be conducive to productivity.

NOT TO BE CONFUSED WITH PERFECTIONISM

It's often confused with doing things perfectly, but striving for consistency is actually the opposite of perfectionism. When you focus on getting through your daily quota of work, or practice, you can't allow yourself to waste time going back over what's gone before, endlessly fine-tuning. You need to press on. Daily targets – time-specific to-do lists – are a great way to ensure you stay focused. Choose whatever constraints work for you: a tick list of tasks; setting a word count for a report you're working on; allocating an hour of your day to thinking about a problem that needs solving (take yourself off somewhere away from your devices to do this if you can).

In her bestselling book on creativity, *The Artist's Way*, written in the '80s, the American writer Julia Cameron champions a consistent approach. She recommends the daily writing of 'morning pages', without fail, first thing on waking. It was an approach she stumbled across as a struggling screenwriter and single mother, and it worked because it required only a small amount of time every day (the target is three pages of longhand, which takes around half an hour for most people). It is a technique that has worked for thousands of people, and her book (and its various spin-offs) have sold in huge numbers.

Cameron's bite-size strategy is encouraging. Consistency can feel particularly difficult to achieve for women with family responsibilities. We are overburdened in general, with demands of children, family, friends and domestic responsibilities that outstrip men's. Urgent needs (that often relate to the welfare of other people who depend on us) trump our own on a daily basis. ONS data from the UK shows that, on average, women still do 60% more 'unpaid work' than men – including the bulk of household caring and housework.[19] But ensuring a commitment requires only the minimum of time makes it more likely we'll be able to stick to it. Perhaps that's why Cameron's method is so popular – it doesn't take up much time.

THE RULE OF REGULAR CONTACT

Anyone who has parented a child who plays an instrument can see the benefits of consistent practice in action. Little and often, even five minutes a day, makes a tangible difference.

Little and often approaches benefit the bottom line in business, too. I remember hearing about an executive named Jim Stallings, who ran the Systems Technology Group Division in IBM. He dramatically increased the revenue of his business when he took over. He told his sales staff he would only be measuring one thing: the volume of calls to potential new clients. He set them a target of ten new calls per week. Simply because they stuck to this and put a consistently higher number of new leads out each week, profits increased. In the past, some sellers had put in more than ten calls, and the figures varied wildly from week to week. But the new regime introduced a consistent approach.

This approach, based on regular contact and perseverance is just as beneficial when it comes to existing clients as it is with new ones. I'm a big believer in keeping in touch and staying front of mind and since I moved into sales I have always encouraged my teams to maintain consistent

---

19. www.visual.ons.gov.uk/the-value-of-your-unpaid-work/

contact with clients. Now, this applies to contact on social media as much as it does to picking up the phone or scheduling meetings. Allocating a consistent amount of time to networking on social media can transform it from another dreaded to-do with unclear benefits into an invaluable sales and marketing tool. But it doesn't work if you are inconsistent about it.

I started my own 5 a.m. waking after reading *The Morning Miracle* by Hal Ellard. In it, he advises dividing the first, early power hour into four segments, and focusing on a different thing for each one. Committing to fight distraction is easier when the circumstances are in your favour. Getting up super-early is one way to ensure this. If it's 5 a.m. and your children aren't awake yet, circumstances are less likely to conspire against you.

I read *The Morning Miracle* at a time when I needed to assimilate a lot of new information relating to my switch from finance to sales and I decided to put some of its recommendations to the test – Ellard is big on breaking tasks down into smaller chunks, so I applied this to a major challenge I was facing. I needed to develop an understanding of a huge range of technical products and their features. The task was extremely daunting. Each product had its own 'red book': a technical manual containing detailed information about the product. There were more than a hundred of them. I felt overwhelmed every time I opened one of them and knew I needed to think of a more creative way to solve the problem.

I approached one of the senior technical staff and asked

him to spend 15 minutes every day face-to-face with me, talking me through key features and elements of each product. The bite-size regularity of these segments of learning made the challenge feel less daunting. Within three months, we had covered the full product catalogue and I understood enough to explain each of our products to a client.

It taught me a lesson about learning. Little and often: concentrating on one small thing at a time works far better than 'learning by firehose'. By scheduling this learning and making it a regular thing, it became part of the rhythm of my day. Once something becomes habituated, it's easy to stick to it and then build up, in increments, whether it's Pilates or practising your sales pitch.

CONSISTENCY HELPS FIGHT THE POWER

By resolving to deliver conscientiously and present a consistent image to your colleagues, there's a surprising upside too: you'll be fighting one of the oldest and most sexist workplace prejudices about women. That old myth that women are emotionally turbulent – inconsistent in terms of our moods and behaviours. This, of course, pits women as erratic and unreliable. Men, in contrast, are solid, constant, to be relied upon, goes the theory. Although it sounds quaintly outdated, harking back to an era when 'hysteria' was a medical *thing*, this view is still alarmingly widespread.

Google 'women and men's moods' and three of the top four headlines speak for themselves:

WOMEN SPEND 10 DAYS A YEAR IN A GRUMPY MOOD

WOMEN BORN TO BE MOODY

WOMEN MOODIER THAN MEN

The simplicity and blatant bias of such articles may be risible, but we shouldn't laugh it off. It all feeds into a climate where gender stereotypes abound. This is despite the fact that science has proved these myths have little foundation in fact. A 2012 review by researchers at the University of Toronto found no conclusive link between the rhythm of women's menstrual cycles and their moods when they reviewed 45 international studies into the subject. PMS has, for years, given the unhelpful mythology around women's perceived 'mood swings' scientific ballast, so with this discovery that the evidence simply isn't there, such generalization begins to look more obviously sexist and lazy.

The myth of the 'moody woman' is one that falls into the same camp as the other aspersions I mentioned that are so often cast at working women, generally with the qualifier of being '*too* much...' of what whatever it happens to be. As we've discussed, there is some truth in the idea that women as a general rule are more compassionate and nurturing than men, but there is no evidence for women having more mood swings than men at work or outside it.

Carbon's Georgina Hill says this unconscious sexism is pervasive: 'Young women entering the workforce often experience this bias, being questioned about their mood when they aren't visibly expressing pure joy and enthusiasm. For women, if you have a straight face in a meeting or at your desk, if you have a natural frown concentration face, men will ask: "What's wrong?" "You look upset", they say, or "Why aren't you happy?" Worst of all, they may just tell you: "Smile". It feels as if they would be more comfortable if you outwardly showed happiness so that they don't feel like you're moody or angry at them. I have had so many times when I've been in meetings, listening to what my male colleague or manager is saying, and them stating "You're not smiling", or "You don't seem happy with that."'

It's hard to imagine a woman asking a man if he was upset because he wasn't smiling during a meeting. If a man has a straight face, he's working, concentrating, focused, even strong. If a woman has a straight face, she's moody, upset, something's wrong, she doesn't like you.

'Consistency doesn't mean consistently happy, or consistently pleasing everybody else,' Georgina adds. 'Consistency is being clear on your objectives and goals and sticking to that as you work. Yes, we already have these stereotypes of being moody, but our job is not to prove these wrong by being cheerful and pleasing everyone. Our job is to be our true selves throughout, keeping a level head.'

The best way we can fight this insidious bias is to behave in a consistent, calm way on a daily basis. Do this, and deliver good work, methodically over time, and you'll be building a personal brand that's resilient and reliable.

AIM FOR AVERAGE SPEED, NOT MAX SPEED

Consistency is also only achieved by keeping a level head, so take a look at the chapter on Calm towards the end of the book. It's really important when you're thinking about consistency to avoid being too self-punishing: 'It's easy to fall into a trap of letting a bad day, an unhealthy meal or an argument define our view of ourselves, even temporarily,' Georgina says. 'Viewing such slip-ups as anomalies and part of the journey can feel like an effort, but it's important to maintain perspective.'

When we're considering the prospect of doing business with another person, it's important to be sure that they'll do what they promised, that their word has value. If we don't, we may lose confidence in them.

'Having worked with a series of inconsistent bosses, who were over-friendly one moment and dismissive the next, changing their mind about priorities and deadlines, I was determined not to be like that when I became a manager,' said one UK-based sales director who asked not to be named.

HOW CONSISTENT ARE YOU?

As part of our approach at Carbon, we've identified some dominant consistency types to help you assess your consistency characteristics. Have a look at the quadrants below and see which one sounds most like you:

Fire-starter	Consistent performer
• Goes off with a bang but fizzles out quickly • Tends to work in bursts and then crash • High output but poor stamina	• Balances high output with frequency • Sets and meets expectations • Highly motivated
Stop-starter	Work-a-day
• Non-committal • Tries a bit but immediately gives up • Easily demoralized, not motivated • Put off by high-engagement tasks	• Tends to stick to what is expected, doesn't push beyond • Frequent and consistent, but poor output • Coasting

Quadrant 1: You do a lot in short bursts. Go to chapters Calm and Clarity to become a Carbon Leader

Quadrant 2: You start out with good intentions but tend to give up easily. Go to chapters Confidence and Character to become a Carbon Leader

Quadrant 3: You do what you have to do. Go to chapters Change and Choice to become a Carbon Leader

Quadrant 4: You're already highly consistent. Go to chapter Community and get involved

Consistency starts from within. If you meet your own small internal expectations, it will build your faith in your ability to achieve more significant things. And remember that success isn't an end goal, it's a process.

Last but not least, when you're managing other people, make sure you give consistent, positive praise. Even when the praise relates to small things, it makes a big difference to morale and performance.

CHANGE

'Progress is impossible without change,
and those who cannot change their minds
cannot change anything.'
George Bernard Shaw

I'VE ALWAYS HAD CHANGE forced upon me. In that, I've been lucky, although it didn't always seem that way. I travelled alone from Dar es Salaam to Canada when I was seven. I was sent to live with my aunt for a few years to experience North American culture.

This unsettling start was a blessing in disguise. It helped me build my confidence. My aunt's house was full of girls – my three cousins (Salima, Shelina and Narmin) and they were all feminists. They all encouraged me to believe I could do anything I set my mind to, but whereas my mother was reluctant to praise, my aunt was a lot more encouraging. I benefited from excellent schooling whilst I was living with her and I built strong relationships with my female cousins. By the time I returned to Tanzania, my confidence had grown enormously. It taught me to regard change with an open mind, and helped me develop an inner strength. I had a newfound faith in myself, particularly in my ability to adapt and thrive outside of my comfort zone.

Most of the time, we approach change with caution. We discuss it, contemplate it, plan for it, visualize it. But sometimes, when we can't do this, we don't give ourselves the chance to talk our way out of it, to rationalize fear into good sense and stay where we are.

Change, which is generally approached as a stage in a linear process, instead becomes a sharp, sudden recalibration followed by a period of fast adaptation, making sense in retrospect rather than projecting forward. The downside of this is that it can cause temporary panic, disorientation and high levels of stress, but for me, the benefits have always outweighed the extra anxiety.

At times, though, it's been a close call. Particularly the time when my then new husband (we had only been married for a year and were in our early 20s) accepted a job and moved us to Paris without consulting me. He told me when we were at the airport flying out! He had led me to believe we were going on a surprise holiday… In fact, unbeknownst to me, he had signed a contract with a French NGO, taking a job for which one of the requirements (we realized when we read the small print), was that his spouse would not be granted permission to work! I remember reading these words in his contract (from my seat on the plane to Paris) and feeling sick. We had a huge argument.

Despite feeling furious and slightly desperate when attempts to renegotiate this part of his contract backfired, I found my old sense of adventure began to kick in once we started to explore our new city. Things got worse before they got better, though. To soften the blow of the enforced move, my husband, Fayyaz, had planned a surprise holiday to Spain immediately after the move, knowing I had always wanted to visit. But just as we were about to leave for the holiday, a crisis in Tajikistan meant his new company needed him to fly there immediately. No holiday to Spain. Meanwhile, we had no apartment in Paris, no bank account and I had no work permit. We were living out of a suitcase, staying in a soulless hotel. The fact that his work trip was likely to be a long one compounded my misery.

After he'd left for the trip, leaving our marriage hanging in the balance, I remember spending a particularly depressing afternoon contemplating my options. I could call it quits, then fly back to Canada and start over again – but really that was not an option given he was the love of my life, or use the opportunity to try something fresh – view it as a challenge, an adventure.

I opted for the latter. I had always wanted to live in Paris, after all. But I became quickly dispirited when my search for a company to offer me work and sponsor me so I could get a visa – proved impossible. It was a catch 22 – no company wanted to offer me work unless I had a visa and I couldn't get a visa without a job. After a week or two of hearing the same bad news, feeling miserable as hell, I decided to spend a few days exploring Paris, hanging out in the cafés and people watching. I was in a café in the city one morning when I heard English voices. They were arguing. I assumed they were tourists who were struggling to communicate something to the waiter and I approached them to offer help, and we got chatting.

It transpired they were arguing about their business – they ran a school and had a key member of staff who was leaving unexpectedly, a chemistry teacher. I said I had been a chemistry major at Cornell. I told them about my work predicament. They exchanged a glance and said: 'Do you think you could teach 7th grade chemistry, starting next week?' I told them I thought could. They asked me to do a trial lesson, which I prepped for, working around the clock for two days to get my lesson plan ready. It went well and they offered me the job. We made a deal. They would sponsor me so that I could get a work visa if I agreed to teach at the school for a year before looking for another job.

It was a total change of course for me, but I jumped at it. It turned out to be one of the most interesting and illuminating 'wrong turns' I've ever made. It was challenging and interesting and I met some great people at the school. I returned to finance after that year in teaching, but the experience taught me some powerful life lessons. Here they are in brief:

- With application and focus, it's possible to become competent at something new quickly.
- There is something joyful about encouraging other people. I saw first-hand the benefits of the encouragement I offered to my students. This experience has informed my management style in subsequent jobs. In order to flourish, everybody needs to feel nurtured.
- Life doesn't always pan out in the way you'd choose, but sometimes something that looks like a step backwards may be a blessing in disguise.

Nineteen years on, it's impossible for me to view our move to Paris as anything other than an absolutely fortuitous fork in the road. I love living here and have had a series of wonderful career opportunities since we moved. The teaching job hasn't been the only one that involved a sideways or seemingly 'backwards' jump either. This experience has led me to broaden my definition of success, and to think less rigidly about my career in general.

Developing a high tolerance for change is, I believe, central to success. In a fast-paced economy, where new technologies are making traditional roles redundant; staying still, and getting stuck in a single process-focused or technical job makes you a target for redundancy in the long term. There's a paradox here: those who try the hardest to stay still and keep hold of their life as it is are the most likely to lose it. Women are particularly likely to fall into this trap, seeking to maintain a status quo in the mistaken belief that it offers more stability in the long run.

I've seen this in my own career. One of the greatest jobs I've had was at IBM. I was Pricing Methodology Manager for the consulting part of the organization. It was a great job. I loved the team, especially my manager, Mike Newsam. Thanks to him, my work was varied and flexible. I worked 9–3.30 four days a week, and Mike reminded me to leave when I wasn't out of the door on time. I remember thinking at the time that in terms of job satisfaction, I'd probably hit a career highpoint. From a work/life point of view it was perfection. A large part of me was tempted to stay put. I can see how this could tempt many women, in particular, to settle. Although this was appealing in one sense, experience has taught me to keep moving.

At Carbon, we advise women who want to be successful to develop a portfolio of skills. This is good advice for everyone. Where possible, it's a smart move to spread yourself across a range of different opportunities. Have a 'bit on the side,' when it comes to work. That way, if one avenue closes, you have other options. Easy to say, perhaps, but also, probably easier than you think to achieve.

Let's look at some examples. You might be thinking, you work full time so any extra work-related commitments are out. But could you volunteer to get involved in a new project at work that falls slightly outside of your usual area? Could you put yourself forward as a mentor, explore opportunities for a new start-up on the side, or act as a consultant on a friend or ex-colleague's new venture? Laurence Haziot, one of my most inspiring female mentors once said to me: 'So long as you're moving, you're increasing your skillset. Once you stay still, it's then that you're at risk of stagnation.'

Another colleague, Brian Mulada, gave me some sound advice about picking next steps in a career. He advised me to look for a new role that had two or three elements that were new, but a couple that were familiar – that I felt already capable of. This is good advice for any change (in so far as it's possible to control – sometimes it isn't).

When I moved into sales, I didn't feel I had this continuity, but my manager, Tony Devore, helped me find it. He sat me down and told me that I knew the company, I knew the products inside out too. The sales-specific expertise was something I would learn on the job. Finding those touch-stones of competence and familiarity really helped me. There was enough of a history for me at IBM to take the risk.

You don't need to be constantly restless and flit from job to job every few months (although don't hang around too long!), but ensuring that you're making progress in different areas of your life will mean that even if you aren't in a new job, you're keeping your skills and attitude fresh by challenging yourself. Keeping one eye on your skills development ensures you're open and aware of new opportunities, too, particularly those that may come from an unlikely direction.

I like to explain this concept using an image of a rope swing. Imagine you're sitting on the swing. A strong rope is made up of individual strands, twisted together. This is what makes it strong, and the more strands, the harder the rope is to break. Even if one or two of the strands wear through, there are enough other fibres to keep the rope from breaking. If you're working to expand your skills, you'll be adding strands as you go along, so any broken strands will soon be replaced with new ones. Your swing will stay up.

The small miracle is that within seven to ten years, the strands in your rope may well be unrecognizable from the original ones, which may have worn through and fallen by the wayside. Strand by strand, you will have totally transformed your life.

At Carbon, when we're working with women who want to work out how to develop and advance, we encourage them to take the long view. I ask them: 'Where do you want to be in seven years' time?' Then we work backwards to establish what they could be doing now to make that a reality. It's less daunting than a five-year plan and the longer timespan encourages people to be more ambitious and to think outside the box about future possibilities. Most senior positions require a breadth of experience. In contrast, those who become experts in one particular field, building technical expertise that is specific, risk becoming specialized that they become indispensable. They have effectively narrowed their prospects by becoming too good at their job. Internally, they get pigeonholed, and may struggle to convince managers that they are capable of other more senior and strategic positions. When it comes to advancement, being a generalist with at least two areas of specialty (M shaped versus T shaped) is an asset.

As a rough guide, aim to stay in a job for three years maximum. Ideally, two years. A report in Forbes found that those who stay within their job for more than two years get paid 50% less over the long run than those who move more frequently.

Moving regularly keeps you fresh. Take a look at the lifecycle of a job chart opposite, and the tips that follow to find out about how to make the best of the phase you're in.

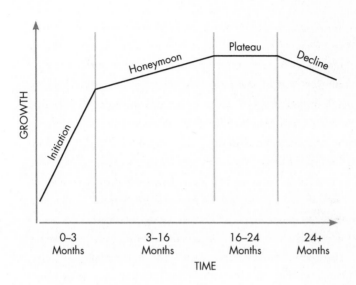

Figure 2: Lifecycle of a Job

0–3 MONTHS: INITIATION

You're learning the ropes. Don't attempt to come in and make major changes from day one, it's important to get the measure of how things have been done up until now, so that you can get a feel for what works and what doesn't.

TOP TIP: Before you start the new job, try to make sure other stresses in your life are dealt with. Hang in there, too, it will only get better.

3–16 MONTHS: HONEYMOON

Ideally, this is when you're starting to feel competent, and can begin to implement changes and bring your fresh perspective to the role. You should be feeling motivated and challenged, and you should be learning.

TOP TIP: Enjoy this! Don't stress for the sake of it.

16–24 MONTHS: PLATEAU

Changes you have introduced should have bedded in. You begin to feel comfortable and competent in the job. You can take challenges in your stride, but you don't feel as challenged or motivated as you did during the honeymoon phase.

TOP TIP: Listen to your gut, you'll know when the time is right to move.

24 MONTHS: DECLINE

You start to lose interest and begin to look around for other opportunities. If you don't move now, you need to find a way to reinvigorate your existing job, by suggesting changes, perhaps taking responsibility for an exciting new project or looking at new ways to add value.

TOP TIP: Can you do this for the rest of your life? If not, move.

During my own career, I've changed roles every 18 months or so, which perhaps leaves too little room for consolidation and has at times been a bit exhausting. This may sound unrealistic for women who are pregnant or have young children. There's an instinct many mothers have to nurture, which often translates into keeping life safe and stable. When you feel vulnerable in your personal life, it may feel crazy to take on anything challenging or risky at work. But when you stop to consider it, there's actually something primal about the need to keep moving to ensure security.

Even in pre-industrial times, change was built in to healthy functioning. Crops would be rotated to ensure the soil had enough nutrients to grow food. Communities needed to be ready to bolt and build a new life if they came under attack. It feels counterintuitive now, with our concept of security tied to conservative ideas about maintaining the status quo, but it's true.

I find that major life changes such as parenthood are a huge life-changing shift that for many, can be a great catalyst for the resetting of boundaries around work and life. It can also prompt you to instigate more flexible and potentially fulfilling work. This doesn't have to equate to the scaled-back part-time roles of days gone by. Scope out your own solution and present it to your company. You may be surprised by the response.

The biggest enemy to change, for most of us, is ourselves. The limiting voice inside your head that cautions you against trying new things, then whispers, when you don't do them, that you were right to hold back. You then see proof of your wisdom everywhere: your cautiousness was wise. Confirmation bias kicks in. By giving in to doubt and closing yourself down, you harness negative, protective energy. This is learnt behaviour, and it perpetuates low confidence. In contrast, pursuing change helps you to build mental and emotional strength. It makes you more resilient. Accepting change and rolling with it creates a virtuous circle. You can only harness the positive energy of change if you aren't fighting it.

But this is harder for women to do, as a general rule. Intentionally or not, society enables men to be the choosers. We expect men to make the decision, to take risks. Women are subconsciously asked to be more understanding, to be gentle, to let others take the lead. In studies on risk-taking behaviour, women perceived more negative outcomes than men. They imagined the fallout of the risk to be more extreme, and more likely than men did.[20] At a deep psychological level, many women are conditioned to believe that other people may be best placed to make decisions for them (somewhat ironic when you consider that studies show higher testosterone levels correlate with impulsive, ill-considered decisions, where men opt to trust instinct over reason).[21]

Women too often strive for comfort. We happily sit in a comfort zone, stay in a comfortable job. We keep safe. Men don't strive for comfort in the same way, they push themselves out of their comfort zone more willingly. This is what we all have to do if we want to keep growing and moving

20. www.journal.sjdm.org/06016/jdm06016.htm

21. www.sciencedaily.com/releases/2017/04/170428154556.htm

forward. When it comes to your career, it really is a case of no pain, no gain.

It seems unlikely that the next generation of mothers, millennials, are going to put their careers in a holding pattern in the way so many have before. Carbon's Georgina Hill says that for her generation nobody expects to stay put for long: 'I see that as something that's really positive about our attitude to work. There's an expectation that we'll keep moving, that we'll always have an eye on what's coming next. We're resistant to being defined in terms of our current job and we recognize that the whole idea of a "job for life" is crazily anachronistic and dull. I know a lot of successful 30-year-olds who have already had six different jobs. Where once this was frowned on, it's now more likely to be celebrated as a sign of ambition, curiosity and drive.'

Georgina explains that this expectation puts the onus on employers to keep new starters challenged and engaged, offering greater incentives and speedier, more visible career development opportunities. A Forbes report stated that 60% of millennials leave a company within three years of joining. It's a shift that is profoundly altering the way we work, and to a certain extent, it's helping to level out old-fashioned 'seen and not heard' pyramid-style management of days gone by. Today's 20-somethings are better adapted for change, too. Millennials entered the workplace shortly after the 2008 crash, so they don't take career stability for granted.

But one area where millennials, like many of the rest of us, struggle, is with developing a clear sense of purpose. We delved into this in our Clarity chapter, but developing a clear view of your ambitions, goals and purpose will ensure you have the strong intuition and confidence you need to pursue the change that best serves you.

In their book *Designing Your Life*, Silicon Valley design engineers Bill Burnett and Dave Evans propose a radical way to rethink the way we approach life. They suggest that many of us are 'working on the wrong problem'. Burnett and Evans explain that, in fact, many people work on the wrong problem for years: grafting away in a job, or career path that can never answer their needs or wants.

Taking time to uncover your purpose, by using the advice in the clarity chapter, should help to shape a sense of direction. Fostering this inspires self-confidence and ensures you become more adaptive to change. When you understand that your purpose is greater than the job you're in currently, or your personal circumstances in any given situation, you are less inclined to cling to the status quo. You're better prepared to see change as the facilitator of new opportunities. Change becomes something to embrace rather than fear.

THREE TYPES OF CHANGE

Change comes in three guises. I want to talk you through them. They are not all created equal, and as I will come to explain, change that you instigate yourself is the most desirable.

1. UNEXPECTED CHANGE

This is the type of change that gets thrown at you. Whether it's moving to a new city for a partner's job, or to care for a sick relative, or your company being merged with another and your team changing, this type of change happens to us all. It's outside of your control and the best thing you can do to prepare for it is to work on your inner confidence and clarity so that when it hits, you can respond from a secure and positive position.

2. BATON CHANGE

This is the type of change that is handed to you. You are picked for a promotion, singled out for some training in a new area of development, or headhunted by an external employer. It's Cinderella change, and it can be great. But the problem is that many women sit around waiting for this to happen and pass up opportunities for proactive change under the misguided belief that a promotion or opportunity will find its way to them if it's 'meant to be'.

3. PROACTIVE CHANGE

This is the best of the bunch. It's change instigated by you. In pursuing change on your own terms, you will be working to develop your intuitive sense of what is right for you. The confidence that springs from this is cumulative, and will help you draw positive change towards you. You can start with baby steps, asking for training or extra responsibility at work, or looking into opportunities abroad, for example. The important thing is to start taking action now.

When it's set out like this, it's easy to see why proactive change is the most desirable. So when the benefits are clear, it's important to look at the things that hold women back from pursuing proactive change. We've established that much of the comfort-zone mentality is informed by fear, particularly fear of failure, so how should we go about challenging that?

Burnett and Evans have an exercise that can help here. It's a way to reframe day-to-day 'failures' and view them as conduits to growth. They suggest the following:

Using the table below, look back over your last week (or month, or year, as you see fit) and log your failures.

Categorize them as screw-ups, weaknesses or growth opportunities.

Identify your growth insights for all of them.

Build a habit of converting failures into growth by doing this once or twice a month.

Failure	Screw-up	Weakness	Growth opportunity	Insight

They say: 'When obstacles happen, when your progress gets derailed, when the prototype changes unexpectedly – life design lets you turn absolutely any change, setback, or surprise, into something that can contribute to who you are becoming personally and professionally.'

Putting yourself out there as someone who is willing to take on change is easier when you take the view that even if an individual job, move or decision doesn't work out, it'll leave you wiser, more enriched and clearer on your goals. 'Failure' on paper doesn't need to mean failure in a bigger-picture sense. Trying new things helps you evolve and keeps life interesting and challenging. And it's OK if sometimes you screw up.

Carbon's Marine Aubin points out that men, in general, are far more comfortable with their screw-ups than women are. 'The men I have worked with are on balance far more OK with their mistakes. They don't really care. The attitude is "Yeah, I'm sorry." Or "Yeah, I screwed up." That's the end of it. They don't talk about it, or pick over what went wrong.' Women tend to take failure far more personally, and research by Harvard's Claudia Goldin found that female students who scored lower than an A in introductory economics were far more likely than male students to switch their major as a result.[22] They decided they weren't up to it rather than persevering to improve their skills and understanding and sticking to their guns.

It feeds back into Malcolm Gladwell's theory of excellence. That it's all about practice: being dogged and

---

22. www.scholar.harvard.edu/files/goldin/files/claudia_gender_paper.pdf

committed and sticking with a new skill until you get good at it. This is something that can easily be done alongside your current job.

I gained a surprising insight into the idea of practising new skills from a senior colleague I had, Remi-Morillon. We stayed in touch after he had retired.

When you stop to consider it, one of life's most extreme changes is retirement. Although it's a luxury increasingly redundant for many, for those who face the prospect of an old-fashioned 'golf and gardening' retirement, the change can be huge. But rather than some of his peers who were struggling with the transition, this particular man explained that he was thoroughly enjoying his retirement because he had planned for the switch, managing it in stages. He had started working on his hobbies, as a side project, for a few years before he stopped work. He gradually slowed his work, going from five days to four, then dropping to three. As a result, there wasn't a terrible shock when he stopped.

He said: 'It's important to decide on what you want to do during your retirement and begin doing it a few years in advance – even a decade in advance. Whether it's golf or creative writing, gardening or volunteering, starting to do a little of it alongside your job means that when the day comes, you'll already be prepared, and feeling enthusiastic about doing more of it!' This is sound advice for anyone anticipating any sort of change in their life. Change doesn't always have to be absolute. You were doing that and now you are doing this. It can build, running alongside your life as it is.

Planning for change proactively is always better than guarding against it and reacting after the event. It ensures you aren't on the back foot, and that you stay aware of opportunities on the horizon.

Just in case you're in the process of deliberating whether to make a leap, knowing you want to be bold but needing an extra push, I'll tell you a little story. When I finished university my first job was with a hedge fund named DE Shaw – as a chemistry major I had no idea what I was getting myself into with derivatives trading. But I took the opportunity presented to me. My first week was emotional as one of the star employees was leaving the company and launching a start-up. I was told he was looking for employees – when I asked what the start-up would specialize in – they said selling books on the Internet, to which I replied 'That'll never work!' Yes, it was Jeff Bezos. My kids call it my billion-dollar mistake. I call it my billion-dollar lesson. Life has a way of giving you plenty of opportunity if you are willing to pivot or change into them.

Don't miss your Amazon moment!

CALM

*'Get yourself grounded and you can navigate even
the stormiest roads in peace.'*
Steve Goodier, writer

CALM IS SUCH A simple word, but it can feel incredibly
elusive. Our lives operate at breakneck speed. We are
constantly 'on', and thanks to technology, work encroaches
on every spare corner of downtime unless we put strict
boundaries around it. But increasingly, research demonstrates that maintaining a sense of calm makes you not
only happier and more content, but better at your job too.
Business is sitting up and taking notice.

It's something that is particularly relevant to women,
as we tend to suffer the effects of stress more acutely than
men. Women are more likely to suffer anxiety and depression than men, and research shows that we can't tolerate
stress hormones as well as men do. Men adapt to stress
hormones by releasing higher levels of adrenocorticotropic
hormone, which triggers the release of cortisol. Their stress
response kicks in quickly and effectively. In contrast, wom-
en's release of stress hormones is described as 'sluggish' – we

have what researchers call 'compromised cortisol feedback'. This lag in stress response is believed to explain, in part, why women are more likely to develop depression when they're under stress.[23]

In a review of research by psychologists at Harvard in 2010, a range of evidence showed that women had evolved a different way of managing stress, too – 'tend and befriend' is characterized by nurturing and networking behaviour during times of stress.[24] In women, these behaviours were found to help reduce levels of stress hormones. So, when you have an urge to phone a friend at the end of a stressful day, you should do it.

For both men and women, burnout is horribly common in the business world. I can think of an alarming number of colleagues over the years who have, at various times and in a range of ways, worked themselves to the point of exhaustion. I approached a number of them to be interviewed for this book, but for understandable reasons, this is a problem that many people want to keep hidden. We're under pressure to be seen to tolerate extreme stress without it impacting on performance.

But the cost of this denial is extreme. After months, and sometimes years, of absorbing stress, one day something gives and they can no longer function. At its most extreme end, this is a life or death problem. We've all seen those headlines – super-high fliers who kill themselves, to the shock and horror of colleagues who hadn't realized

---

23. www.ncbi.nlm.nih.gov/pmc/articles/PMC3425245/

24. www.scholar.harvard.edu/marianabockarova/files/tend-and-befriend.pdf

how much their workmate was suffering. These unfortunate people are the victims of a culture that tolerates dysfunctional levels of stress and expects way too much of its workforce.

In every company I've worked for, there has been a proportion of the staff signed off on long-term sick leave at any one time. It's so common, that it's become the norm. This is something that has got worse in recent years. Where once large businesses used to operate with a surplus of people to work – a ratio of 1.5–1.7 people for every job, which allowed for back-up, vacations etc., now it seems as if the norm is 0.6–0.7. As a result, we are all at least 30–40% overworked. There is no slack in the system, and we're paying the price with our mental health.

Stress and anxiety have become a daily reality for many – something to be managed and lived with rather than overcome. Our tolerance to stress builds over time, so it's easy to build a tolerance to it but if you fail to recognize the signals that things are reaching crisis point. This is bad news for individual wellbeing, but it's bad news for business too. When we're stressed out, levels of the hormones cortisol and adrenaline are elevated.

The body's 'fight or flight' system is primed for attack when stress hormones take over. When you're flooded with these chemicals, the amygdala, the part of your brain responsible for your emotional response to stimuli (with the sole objective of ensuring your survival), takes charge. This process makes reasoned thought, listening and a calm, measured response to whatever the work day throws at you virtually impossible.

'In 2015, after almost four years working as a consultant, I realized that I had spent two years in a job that wasn't enough anymore,' says Carbon's Marine Aubin. 'Although I worked hard, it wasn't stimulating, I was bored and, most of all, the company had evolved in a way that no longer fitted my values. I was constantly stressed, with symptoms such as a racing heart, breathlessness and in the end, panic attacks. At its worst, I would burst into tears when I entered the building and I had panic attacks just choosing my outfits. I had already had two mini-burnouts prior to this so this time around, I recognized the signs my body was sending me and I took some time off... Once again, this was too little too late. It took me a few months and a change of company to fully recover. The way I had been living was unsustainable. We all must learn to listen to what our body is telling us, and heed the early warning signs. It's a powerful barometer for what the mind's deeply feeling.'

Businesses are waking up to the fact that this sort of endemic stress doesn't serve them. 'Wellbeing is the only way to maximize not just happiness but fulfilment and productivity, creativity and, yes, profit. It's the only sustainable way forward not just for individuals but for companies too,' says Arianna Huffington, who has introduced meditation rooms at The Huffington Post. And far from being considered wacky, investing in wellbeing is now seen as a marker of good business sense.

Companies from McKinsey to Google, Apple, Nike and Procter & Gamble all have meditation spaces and promote mindfulness practice within their workforce. At Pitney Bowes' head office in Stamford there is a wellness room. It was created, the HR team tell me, to help facilitate creative thinking. It's a calm space where workers can retreat for a few moments of quiet reflection whenever they need to. It is well used, and managers encourage staff to use it as and when they need it.

All of this is great, and an indicator that a much-needed shift is happening in workplaces around the world. But the responsibility for wellbeing lies with the individual. Whatever your employer's stance on work-life balance, mental health and stress, it's up to individual employees to commit to a calm practice and stick with it. Employers can facilitate this, but the success of any such programme depends on the commitment of the individuals.

Increasingly, studies are showing that even after a relatively short intervention, adopting a regular mindfulness practice can have an impressive impact on concentration, productivity and focus. A German study also found adopting a mindfulness practice was also associated with higher levels of job satisfaction and better regulation of emotions.[25]

Despite reading about the benefits, I found it too tricky to find time to meditate until recently. It was one of those things I knew I ought to do, but never managed to commit to. That was until I began to get up an hour early. You'll have heard about the benefits of early rising, and we explored the 'morning miracle' in our Clarity and Consistency chapters. Everyone from CEOs such as Padmasree Warrior to

---

25. www.researchgate.net/profile/Hugo_Alberts/
publication/234018520_Benefits_of_Mindfulness_at_Work_The_Role_
of_Mindfulness_in_Emotion_Regulation_Emotional_Exhaustion_and_
Job_Satisfaction/links/56d96ecd08aee73df6cf52c3.pdf

celebrities such as Michelle Obama are advocates of the 5–6 a.m. power hour. I decided to adopt it myself after listening to Robin Sharma talk about it. He calls it the 'magic hour', and I've really come to believe it's just that.

Lots of people are put off by the 5 a.m. habit. When you're used to waking up at 7 a.m., it feels far too big an adjustment. If this is the case for you, I recommend working back slowly in increments. Set your alarm 15 minutes early the first week, then move backwards in 15-minute increments until you've habituated a wake-up time that ensures you have a peaceful hour undisturbed before the day starts. This needs to be a time before children are up. Ensure your partner doesn't disturb you either.

There are some other golden rules. No looking at a device of any sort. Do not check your email or your social media feed as soon as you wake up. The objective of this hour is to use it to cultivate a deep sense of calm and clarity that will see you through the rest of the day. It should be sacred, and you should guard against any intrusion on it.

15 MINUTES' MEDITATION

I divide my magic hour into four segments. I spend the first 15 minutes sitting quietly in my living room with my eyes closed, focusing on my breath. I've been doing this for about a year now, but I was shocked by how tough it was to get the hang of at first. I'd find myself distracted almost immediately, my head filling automatically with thoughts. Then I got into a vicious cycle where I felt angry with myself for being distracted.

I quickly realized that my assumption that I'd easily be able to meditate for 15 minutes from day one was faulty. Instead, I decided to build up my meditation time. Like most other things, I realized, meditation takes practice. I started with one-minute baseline, adding an extra ten seconds every day (I used a timer on my phone to tell me when time was up). I kept this up, adding 30 seconds at a time after the first week, and kept going until I got to 15 minutes. Now I'm able to keep my focus on my breath for the full time. It is wonderful to feel so at peace, and to know that for a short time every morning, I can fully clear my mind.

Towards the end of my meditation, I mentally list the things that I'm grateful for. I really believe that this gratitude practice has improved my overall outlook, making me more optimistic about my life in general. Your brain feeds off its self-talk. Remind it of positive messages by checking in with the things that are going well for you, and you will be feeding a wellspring of positivity that will inform the way you view everything.

On the days when I don't manage to do my morning meditation, the difference is obvious. I'm less calm, more distracted. I really feel the benefit of this short breathing meditation, which has taught me to stick with it.

I've also found that some of my most creative ideas come straight after I've meditated. Focusing on the breath rather than the constant stream of thoughts allows the subconscious mind space to breathe. I'm a big believer in the often-repeated self-help wisdom that we all have the answers we need within us, and that finding them is more a question of tapping into innate wisdom rather than seeking it from the outside in.

Research shows that mindfulness meditation improves creative thinking. In a study by researchers at Leiden University, meditation led to improvements in divergent thinking (thinking up as many possible solutions for a given problem).[26] Individuals who meditated for 25 minutes before an assessment saw a significant improvement in their capacity to think around a problem. For anyone feeling sceptical about the work-related benefits of the practice, this gives a pretty powerful motivation. What business doesn't want its staff to think up fresh ways to approach the problems it faces?

The remaining three 15-minute segments of my hour run as follows:

15 MINUTES READING

This must be something unrelated to work. It could be a novel, a self-help book, or an in-depth news article that interests me. At the moment, I'm reading about political history as it's a passion for both my husband and my son, and I want to be able to join in with their conversations. Sometimes, the reading may be something tangentially related to work, but I don't allow myself to pick up anything that relates to my existing to-do list. Talking of which…

---

26. www.sciencedaily.com/releases/2014/10/141028082355.htm

15 MINUTES PRIORITIZING

I spend the next 15 minutes writing a list of the three major things I want to achieve that day. I've learnt from experience that doing this stops me from doing a little of everything and getting nothing done. Setting priorities for myself makes it easier to approach the day with equanimity, plus it's helpful when it comes to setting boundaries too. It's easier to say no to extra requests when I've defined my work scope for the day and know I need to stick to it. I set the firm intention of having finished two of the three tasks by lunchtime. This is because by 1 p.m., the US has woken up and my inbox is deluged with fresh requests from head office.

15 MINUTES OF EXERCISE

I do a mini workout. Usually, this is 15 minutes of HIIT training, or 15 minutes of yoga-based stretching. It isn't much, but because I struggle to fit a full workout in, it really makes a difference to my fitness – over the course of the week it adds up to almost two hours. Also, it's over quickly!

It's important to build calm practices into the everyday too. This is hard to do, particularly if the workplace culture in your office is heads down, nobody takes a lunchbreak and you sometimes find your diary so packed with back-to-back calls and meetings there is no time to stop.

STEP AWAY FROM YOUR DESK

But as with meditation, all the evidence shows that taking regular breaks, particularly leaving the office, benefits concentration, productivity and wellbeing in the long run. A 2014 study found that the ideal ratio was 17 minutes of break to every 53 minutes of work.[27] But although this is unlikely to be realistic in the average office, there is plenty of evidence to show that pausing little and often is better than, say, a long lunchbreak in the middle of the day. It figures: adult attention span ranges from 15 to 40 minutes. Taking care not to over-tax your brain means you'll be more likely to get the full benefit of it when you really need to focus.

I'm a big believer in the benefits of leaving the office. Even a short 10-minute walk outside to grab lunch can be incredibly restorative. The act of removing yourself from your desk gives you physical distance that brings with it intellectual perspective. Research shows that even a gentle lunchtime stroll boosts mood and improves stress tolerance. In a 2015 study by researchers from Birmingham University, where a group of office workers (mainly middle-aged women) took a half-hour lunchtime stroll most days, daily questioning revealed that they felt more enthusiastic, less tense and better able to cope in the afternoons when they had walked.[28]

I used to be a big coffee and diet coke drinker. Reaching

27. www.themuse.com/advice/the-rule-of-52-and-17-its-random-but-it-ups-your-productivity

28. www.ncbi.nlm.nih.gov/pubmed/25559067

for one of these was the punctuation of my day. But when I gave up caffeine (although I do still drink decaf coffee), I switched to walking breaks. I have colleagues who take breathing breaks in the office, but I have to escape the physical environment for 10 to 15 minutes. For me, that's part of the power. A short walk always gives me a burst of energy and fresh perspective. It gets the blood flowing and allows me to come at a problem with fresh eyes.

It's often the case that the best ideas come out of context. When you're trying to solve one problem, sitting with it and worrying away is rarely the answer. Counterintuitively, focusing on something completely different for an hour instead of going over the same old ground, can give you a jolt that enables you to view the original problem with renewed calm and perspective.

A colleague of mine, Laura Miragoli, (head of Operations for Microsoft Italy) used to say, 'Shemin, you need to take a proper lunch break – it is better for your mind and better for your work!' And being a great friend she would often drag me out and, being Italian, we always ate well! The year that we worked together was the year I began to make the leaps in career due to the breakthrough ideas we came up with during our lunch break.

Taking yourself out of context creates a space for fresh ideas. When you're trying to solve something, rather than worrying it over and thinking around it in your head, try thinking about something totally different. When you do this, inspiration and fresh perspective are more likely to flow. For me, giving my full attention to a conversation that has nothing to do with work (such as the discussions I have with my husband and son about history) works as a positive distraction. I always feel mentally invigorated after these conversations.

Occasionally, I'm aware of a nagging voice in the back of my mind telling me that I have unfinished business waiting for me on my computer, but I've got better at ignoring unhelpful worries, and guilt.

GUILT: THE ENEMY OF CALM

Guilt seems to be an emotion that's problematic for women, and for working women in particular. It's such a negative emotion, no good comes of it and it breeds anxiety and stress. We talked about this a bit in a previous chapter, but the classic bind is that working women feel guilty that they aren't home more, and simultaneously guilty that they can't devote the same energy to their job that they brought to it pre-motherhood. In the past, I have felt this acutely, and residual guilt became so ordinary for me that it spilt over into all sorts of other areas of my life. I'd feel guilty that I had more money than other people; guilty for not working in the evening; guilty for not being a good parent; guilty for not being a good daughter. I even felt guilty for going on holiday.

Thankfully, one of the many things that living in France has really helped me to do is to take proper vacations and switch off. This is a big part of the French culture, and it's widely expected that even the most senior members of staff in an organization need three weeks to decompress in the summer. When everybody works such long hours, under considerable pressure to deliver, it takes most of the first week of a holiday to switch off. And for the three or so days before the return to work, it is on your mind again.

There's a word for a relaxing pause in French: *détente*. I think of this as a kind of suspended animation, and it's something we all need.

At a micro level (and between holidays), *détente* can come from quality sleep. Ensuring the conditions are conducive each night to give your body the best chance of calm and restorative rest, is a sound investment in your mental health, and your general ability to function both in and outside of work.

SLEEP: THE FOUNDATION OF CALM

In Arianna Huffington's book on sleep, she argues that going to work on too little sleep is, physiologically speaking, pretty much akin to going to work slightly tipsy. Recent research shows that moderate sleep deprivation produces impairments equivalent to those of alcohol intoxication.[29] After 17 to 19 hours without sleep, performance is the same or worse as it is when subjects have a blood alcohol concentration of 0.05%. After longer periods without sleep, performance matches levels equivalent to 0.1% blood alcohol, which is over the drink drive limit.

This, of course, would be unethical, not to mention risky and crazy for anyone wanting to do their job to the best

---

29. www.ncbi.nlm.nih.gov/pmc/articles/PMC1739867/pdf/ v057p00649.pdf

of their abilities. It's an effective demonstration of the need to take sleep more seriously. The science of sleep is inexact. Everybody is different in terms of their sleep needs, but for most of us seven hours or so is a healthy minimum and the sleep we get in the earlier part of our sleep cycle is the most valuable.

Huffington is a fan of sleep rituals (and so are many sleep experts). People who struggle with insomnia are often encouraged to work on their 'sleep hygiene' to help get their body clock back under control. Major no-nos are blue light from devices in the two hours before bed. Likewise, strenuous exercise just before bed is a bad idea, leading to an elevated heart rate in the first few hours of sleep for that night.[30] In contrast, calming activities such as lengthy baths, listening to a podcast or reading a non-work related book can help to relax your mind.

I don't have a bathtub, but I find drinking something hot and non-caffeinated and reading something not related to work does the trick for me. I do this religiously, and won't check my email after 9 p.m. unless the circumstances are exceptional. I have noticed a marked improvement in my sleep quality since I began to stick with my regime. It really helps me to wind down and switch off, so that when I climb into my bed, I'm primed for a calm night's sleep.

Fostering a sense of deep inner calm may sound a bit wishy-washy, but the benefits are hard to argue with. In addition to the boost to your productivity, creativity and focus (and the decline in stress, anxiety and overwhelm),

---

30. www.ncbi.nlm.nih.gov/pubmed/20673290

cultivating calm is great for your personal brand. When you seem unflappable, serene under pressure and in control, you'll look more like a leader, too. When a difficult meeting gets heated, an inner calm will help you to keep your cool: it's the perfect antidote to any of those myths about women being 'over-emotional' in business.

Keen to get started? Here is a simple everyday calm practice, created by Isabelle Rigaud-Mallet. She learnt about the importance of mindfulness the hard way following an exhausting stint working seven days a week as a brand consultant. After realizing something had to give, Rigaud-Mallet discovered meditation and guided breathing. She has recently set up her own holistic coaching company, Be Lively.

Rigaud-Mallet recommends integrating these three practices into your day. Aim to do all three over the course of each day for best results. But even one will make a difference.

THREE TO FIVE MINUTE GUIDED BREATHING:

Breathe in slowly and deeply, allowing the breath to fill your belly, then your ribcage, rising up to your clavicle. Exhale slowly, imagining you are filling an imaginary balloon as you do so. Exhale every last bit of air from your lungs before you breathe in again.

THREE TO FIVE MINUTE MINDFULNESS MEDITATION:

Put your hand into your bag and pull an object out of it. Whatever it is, focus on it intently. Notice everything about it, and think about how you would describe it to an alien.

THREE TO FIVE MINUTE SANCTUARY ANCHORING

Create a mind sanctuary by building a visualization of a place where you feel deeply relaxed and safe. Imagine an exact place, whether it's a beach you love, or a beautiful garden. It should feel like an oasis. Imagine yourself there and use your senses to conjure up the details. Imagine your bare feet touching the sand or the grass. What can you hear, smell, see? If it's a real place you visit often, take a short video one day when you're there to help you recall the details. The more you practise the visualization, the more vivid it becomes.

Rigaud-Mallet's final word on calm is powerful. Rather than a specific exercise, it's a recommendation to rethink the way we regard the impact of stress and trauma on ourselves. 'The Japanese have a philosophy, Kintsugi. The term refers to the technique of mending cracked and damaged porcelain with a glaze that contains gold. The effect makes a feature of the fissures rather than attempting to disguise them and the "mended" object often ends up more beautiful for it. A good calm practice is like the gold glaze – it turns our breaks into blessings, helping us to restore ourselves to serenity with renewed wisdom and a deeper and more robust understanding of ourselves. As a result, we are stronger and more wonderful.'

It is perfectly possible to strengthen your sense of inner calm without investing great amounts of time and without having to radically rethink your life. The best way to introduce a calm practice is to think slow and small. A few minutes here and there really can have a powerful impact on the way that you think and feel.

COMMUNITY

'If you want to go fast, go alone.
If you want to go far, go together.'
African proverb

I'D LIKE TO START this chapter by sharing an unlikely story. It's about chickens. But I think it teaches us something deep and revelatory about human beings. Four years ago, in the US, evolutionary biologist William Muir of Purdue University decided to see if he could increase the productivity of the average flock of battery chickens by selecting the birds from each cage that were the most prolific layers (all the cages had nine hens in them, and he chose one from each, reproducing only the 'super chickens'). He repeated the process over a number of generations. The final results were shocking.

'I' ONLY WORKS WITH A 'WE' BEHIND IT

Rather than creating a flock of birds guaranteed to deliver, the result was the opposite, and the effect got progressively worse in subsequent generations. By the end of the experiment (generation 6), all but three of the chickens in the 'super chicken' group were dead. This was because the surviving chickens had pecked one another to death. The selection of 'the best' hens had led to a generation of hyper-aggressive birds. Conclusion: the most productive hens in each cage at the outset were the biggest bullies, who achieved their productivity partly by suppressing the other birds. The second group of hens (where Muir selected the best cage out each time, to breed from) were overwhelmingly healthy, and they were producing eggs at a far more efficient rate than they had been at the outset of the experiment. Selecting the most prolific group, it turns out is far more effective than selecting the most prolific individual.

In her 2015 TED talk, 'Forget the Pecking Order at Work', Margaret Heffernan, entrepreneur, former CEO of five companies and author, referenced the chicken study, then compared it to research by academics at MIT, where the productivity of different groups of workers was studied. The groups who performed best had neither the highest aggregate IQ, nor the most exceptionally bright individual members. Instead, they had three things in common. They showed a high degree of social sensitivity to one another and they gave equal time to one another – no one voice dominated. The more successful groups also had more women in them.

Old-fashioned corporate thinking (and much of education) has in the past been overly focused on individuals. 'At school, it's the case that if you "keep your head down" and "work hard" your efforts will be rewarded. You'll get an A,' says Carbon's Georgina Hill. 'You don't need to collaborate with anyone else to do this and you don't need to stick your neck out either. But the rule doesn't apply in business.'

In the workplace, although individual 'stars' shine brightly, they do so in a context where there are a mixture of skills and where star performers form one part of a natural ecosystem that supports and enables them. This proves that 'community' in the workplace is far from an airy-fairy idea. In actual fact, a strong community benefits the bottom line. There are a number of studies that show that group incentives are more effective than individual incentives when it comes to increasing workplace productivity – in research at Washington University, moving from individual to group incentives led to a boost of 14% in overall productivity.

This is a crude demonstration of the fact that humans are naturally collaborative – we don't want to let our side down. The flip side of this is that through showing care to other people, we also get to bask in reflected glory. I remember Angela Pisano, a wonderful friend of mine and one of the first people I worked with at IBM, saying to me: 'When I watch the women I've supported over the years go on to do great things, I always feel pride. I share in their success. It's my success too.' I think this is a wonderful way to view mentoring. We should all think in this way. Angela helped me build my network and find my bearings in the sea of processes at IBM and I owe much of my success there to her as a result.

Not all women are as lucky. There is still a sizeable minority of senior women around who don't subscribe to this view. They are still stuck in the old-fashioned mindset that says: 'I've had to pay my dues and so should you.' These may be women in senior positions who have had to compromise their family life, cope without peer support, and 'man-up', in order to get to where they are. Some of them feel that other women should be made to do the same. I experienced this before I joined IBM. I remember, in early job interviews with investment banks, having the sense I was being 'hazed' by a sorority who were fierce and hard to please.

They set horrible challenges designed to make new recruits embarrass themselves, like asking me to open a window that was painted shut. I was also told to take boxing lessons to become more aggressive. It was horrible and demoralizing. What's more, behaving in this unsupportive way makes no sense when it comes to business. It's counterproductive for the women themselves and impedes the contribution and progress of new women entering the business. It's the same mentality you see in schoolgirls who set themselves apart saying: 'I'm not like other girls.' It may feel (or look) like the ultimate in empowerment and the rejection of limiting gender stereotypes, but in fact, it's insidious misogyny in a cunning disguise.

In the '70s, researchers at the University of Michigan surveyed 20,000 women and found that those who achieved success in male-dominated environments were at times likely to oppose the rise of other women. They coined the term 'Queen Bee Syndrome' and theorized it was the consequence of patriarchal workplace culture that meant women who made it to the top were obsessed about maintaining their position.[31] Since, studies have shown that

---

31. www.workplacebullying.org/wsj-5/

40% of workplace bullies are women, whilst another study has found that female workplace bullies direct their negative behaviour toward other women 80% of the time. In a survey by the American Management Association, 95% of female managers said they had been undermined by another woman in their career. It can feel as if you're back in high school when you encounter this anti-sisterhood.

Thankfully, current movements in feminism mixed with a more liberal approach to corporate management style is combatting this outdated behaviour. Sometimes, it's simply coming from a misguided place ('I had to graft to get here and so should you' – the idea that the corporate jungle is a tough place and everyone needs to learn that the hard way). To young women starting their careers, though, it may appear as if Queen Bees are scared the new guard are after their jobs. I've had to explain this many times to female staff reports over the years, telling them that most top female managers are not always insecure, it's more that they think it's important that other women learn the hard way, like they did.

Thankfully, the whole idea of 'manning-up' in order to get on at work; to cultivate an image of strength and win leadership roles now seems outmoded. An appearance of strength is important in a leader, but having a range of leadership styles at your disposal is better than being rigidly wedded to old-school alpha dominance. Leadership style depends on the context, it needs to be appropriate to the business culture but also to individual situations. A landmark 2000 HBR (Harvard Business Review) study by Daniel Goleman followed 3,000 mid-level managers over a three-year period and discovered a range of management styles.[32] The effectiveness of these styles varied according to the situational demands of the role and the needs of the business.

'It's understandable that some women currently on boards or in the later stages of their careers feel that this is still the only way to the top, but the latest leadership research shows this just isn't the case.' says Carbon's Georgina Hill. As the journalist Leigh Buchanan, who has written extensively on management, has said, the most highly rated leadership traits now tend to be the more traditionally 'feminine' ones. These include the ability to nurture, support colleagues, show humility and act with empathy.

THE COMMERCIAL CASE FOR THE SISTERHOOD

A 2011 study by Zenger Folkman of data relating to 7,280 male and female leaders found that when they were evaluated by their reports, on 12 of the 16 competencies that define outstanding leadership, female leaders outperformed the men.[33] They didn't just score more highly when it comes to traditionally 'feminine' traits such as nurturing relationships, either. They also outperformed men when it came to taking the initiative and getting results.

What's even more fascinating is that for the one measure where men significantly outscored women (strategic thinking),

---

32. www.hbr.org/product/leadership-that-gets-results/an/R00204-PDF-ENG

33. www.zengerfolkman.com/media/articles/ZFCo.
WP.WomenBetterThanMen.033012.pdf

when the researchers controlled for the fact that this was a trait that was likely to increase towards the top of a business's hierarchy, the picture shifted. As we know all too well, there are more men than women at the uppermost levels of business. But when the survey results adjusted for this, men and women scored the same for strategic thinking, too.

It's widely accepted that collaboration and cooperation are desirable in a business context. Pooling contacts, skills and perspectives is preferable to working in silos. The highs of a project are more exciting when they're shared, and the lows are less demoralizing. But there's more to it than that. For a start, there's the cross-pollination that occurs when you collaborate with a group of people who have different mindsets, skill sets and networks to you. The benefits of this may be hard to quantify, but academics are getting there. A study by researchers at MIT on call centre workers at a major bank, makes for fascinating reading.[34] In the company studied, productivity between teams varied wildly despite no obvious reason for it. But once they questioned all the teams, they found that the highly successful team had a number of key things that made it different. They spent more time together outside of work, they had stronger bonds and they reported individual relationships within the team and not just with their manager. Once the call centre introduced interventions to create an environment where this could be fostered (whole teams taking their breaks at the same time, instead of on a rota basis), productivity followed. Once the

34. www.sloanreview.mit.edu/article/measuring-the-benefits-of-employee-engagement/

team became more of a community, they became far more effective.

Here is the list of the characteristics shared by successful teams, drawn up by HBR researchers using the data from this study and also information from high-performing teams across a range of other disciplines:
1. Everyone on the team talks and listens in roughly equal measure, keeping contributions short and sweet.
2. Members face one another, and their conversations and gestures are energetic.
3. Members connect directly with one another – not just with the team leader.
4. Members carry on back-channel or side conversations within the team.
5. Members periodically break, go exploring outside the team, and bring information back.

When I met Marine and Georgina, and we decided to form Carbon, there was a lot of cross-pollination. Marine comes with a wealth of experience and contacts that are really different to my own. Georgina brings a fresh perspective and an insight into what it's like for young women right now. Together, we have a perspective that helps to make us stronger together than we are individually. Diversity of perspective, in business as in life, brings strength. The best ideas come out of collaborative thinking.

Marine Aubin says she's seen this over and over during her career, working in a number of start-ups as well as in banks and a range of tech businesses. 'Not only do more points of view deliver richer ideas, but diversity of perspective also strengthens existing ideas. With a range of insights, it's far easier to identify key flaws about something (whether it's a business model, product, proposition or a change of strategy). This enables you to improve and adapt whatever it is that's under consideration.'

With remarkable consistency, data confirms that communication plays a critical role in building successful teams. The HBR study at MIT and others like it found that this positive communication was as significant as a host of other factors combined (the list includes individual intelligence, personality, skill, and the substance of discussions). Pretty impressive, and reason enough for every business leader to look seriously at what they can do to foster inclusive, diverse and integrated teams.

MENTORING MATTERS

One intervention that can help to nurture an inclusive and positive environment is sponsorship and mentoring. 'Structured support by senior colleagues is crucial for women like me who are starting out,' says Georgina Hill. 'Senior women who are successful can have a profound impact on more junior women by helping to guide us. Before I had my current job, I hadn't realized how much of a feminist I was. My generation has been told we can do anything, but then we leave university, join a company and see that almost all the people who have made it to the top are men. The real world workplace can feel retrogressive. Having a senior woman to guide new starters through their first years in the workplace is a great way to help manage this difficult transition.'

Increasingly, there's a move towards sponsorship, as opposed to mentoring, too. In her book *Forget a Mentor, Find a Sponsor*, Sylvia Ann Hewlett, economist, bestselling author and founding President and CEO of the Center for Talent Innovation, a non-profit think tank based in the US, says: 'Mentors advise, sponsors act.' In her research, women who were sponsored were 19% more likely to feel happy about the pace of their progress through an organization than those who did not have a sponsor.[35]

'Mentors give advice; sponsors give capital,' says Marine Aubin. 'Whether that's contacts, opportunities or visibility. They offer something tangible that sponsees can use. At first, this happens organically, the same way Shemin sponsored me. But a programme of sponsorship or mentoring is a great way to nudge a company to do more. The problem with this is that as humans, we're more likely to sponsor people who are like us. That's why senior men are more likely to sponsor men like them (so as a general rule, white men get preference). Some organizations are trying to combat this implicit bias by asking senior executives to nominate two potential sponsors – one male and one female – when they introduce formal sponsorship programmes.'

I'm still benefiting from mentoring. Johnna Torsone, Pitney Bowes's Chief HR Officer, offered to become my mentor and sponsor when I joined. She has helped me

---

35. www.wearethecity.com/wp-content/uploads/2014/10/The-Sponsor-Effect.pdf

understand the dynamics of the business and has provided invaluable advice on a number of occasions. Her Women's Inclusion Network within Pitney Bowes does the same thing for countless other women, too.

LEARNING TO LOVE NETWORKING

How many times have you heard a colleague (or even yourself) saying: 'I hate networking.' Although there are those who relish it, for others it can be tainted with associations of neediness, embarrassment and general uncoolness. But we need to re-frame it. For women who don't have a mentor or a sponsor, it can open up a whole range of opportunities that would otherwise be off limits. Networking is just another word for relationship-building, something that women, to make a sweeping generalization rooted in fact, are more likely to excel at.

Entrepreneur and physician Cécile Monteil's career has been hugely enhanced by networking. In fact, she has become so passionate about the power of networking that she has set up a network of her own: Eppocrate. 'Before I made the move into e-health, I was working full time as a medical doctor, doing my residency. I was passionate about technology and full of ideas. I can honestly say I would never have made the leap if it wasn't for Sandbox (sandbox.is), a network of international influencers who come together to share ideas and inspiration. I was invited to join, and it really expanded my perspective and my sense of what was possible for me career-wise.

'Through the conversations I had with other Sandboxers,

particularly Rand Hindi, one of Sandbox's founders, I was inspired to make the leap to work part-time in a medical tech start-up. I joined the team behind an app: Ad Scientiam, while continuing to work three days a week as a medical doctor.

'Whereas my colleagues in the medical world were sceptical that there were exciting possibilities for mobile phone healthcare technology, tending to pick holes in my ideas, the people I met through Sandbox encouraged me and offered practical advice.'

After leaving Ad Scientiam, Cécile joined iLumens, an innovative organization that offers training through simulation services to better prepare healthcare professionals to practise. At that time, she was also inspired to set up Eppocrate in 2015 – designed to connect medical professionals to entrepreneurs in order to facilitate cross-pollination and the development of new medical technology. The network now has over 2,400 members. Cécile says, 'Our members have found jobs and co-founders, started businesses and developed successful products using the contacts they have made through Eppocrate.'

Hearing stories such as Cécile's makes it all the more frustrating that networking has a bad rap. When it can be a force for positive change, it seems crazy that so many women opt out of it. Marine Aubin experienced the negative perception first-hand when she organized the first networking event for Girlz In Web in 2011. 'Of the 30 women there, 90% had never been to a networking event before,' she says. 'Many of them just didn't see the point of networking (it had been a Girlz In Web battle for a few years). The others were intimidated by the idea. They had no idea of how to do it.'

These commonly reported obstacles helped Marine think about how to create an event that would ensure women would feel supported and welcome. 'I wanted to create a safe space for women to start with networking. Many of the women I talked to when we were planning the event told me they would feel much less judged in a women-only networking event. We understood this. Then, I figured, after a few times, having seen how it works and learnt a few tricks, they would feel 'ready' to go to mixed event... This is exactly what happened, Now I see those women from our first networking event at the most well-known events in France. They are confident and at ease, and many have become more influential as a result.'

And within our board (12 people), 75% changed job within a year thanks to this newfound confidence. Same goes for Lean In where two-thirds of the women make a positive career move after joining a Lean In circle.

This approach, using a women's network as a strategic gateway for broader career advancement, really works. Having a supportive framework helps women build confidence to network effectively in a gender-balanced context going forward. Women's networks are not sufficient to solve the problem of inequality and have met with some criticism within the business community. Some have dismissed them as box-ticking exercises that distract from the real problem: the full and equal integration of both genders in the workplace, right the way up through the organization – 'Supporting the advancement of a gender-balanced workforce' is their mission.

In response, organizations such as London-based HSBC have set up 'balance' networks rather than exclusively female ones, designed to improve integration of men and women. This less 'exclusive' approach is more likely to resonate with younger women, believes Georgina Hill. 'There's definitely an image problem with women's networks for people my age,' she explains. 'Many young women entering the work-force now wish to make it clear from day one that they support workplace equality, and we know that that conver-sation must involve men. That's why balance networks can seem more appealing.'

So, women's networks are useful for building confi-dence and sharing ideas, and they're a helpful space to come together to discuss the unique challenges facing women in the workplace. There's value in doing this without men pres-ent. But when it comes to creating communities that are aimed at making change and progress towards equality, men must come into the equation.

In general terms, we need to stop regarding networking as strictly transactional: that idea that you go to an event look-ing for a new contact to move your career forward. It's this assumption that puts so many people off. Done well, net-working is reciprocal, lateral and natural. It's a way to find out what's going on in your industry (and outside it) and discover how other people have achieved their success. The hope is that their stories might inspire you to think differently about your own. Networking is also a way to build friendships, to share and to listen. It's best to think of it as a long-term pro-ject. Don't expect the benefits to be obvious immediately. But don't doubt that it's worth it. As Sheryl Sandberg says: 'An all business approach is not necessarily good for business.'

CARBON'S FIVE WAYS TO NETWORK LIKE A PRO

DO YOUR RESEARCH

Find out who else is likely to be at an event and read up on them. Where possible, make contact before the event and say you'd like to schedule a chat. Work out exactly what it is you want to get out of it (a piece of advice, their email address, whatever), but then approach them in as relaxed and human a way as possible. In short…

AVOID THE HARD SELL

Because nobody enjoys being obviously pitched at. It's this sort of approach that gives 'networking' a bad name. The likelihood is, an obvious pitch (unless the person you just met invites it) will be inappropriate. Keep the conversation light and as social and relaxed as possible. Ask them questions, tell them if there's something about them you admire or are interested in.

NETWORK WITH EVERYONE

You never know who might be important to you in the future. Often, the best contacts are those who are more slow burn than instant gratification. In the current work climate, people move around a lot. You never know where some-body will be this time next year, or how quickly they might ascend the corporate ranks. Respond with a consistent level of interest and engagement whoever it is you're speaking to, and take care never to appear dismissive or rude.

DECIDE ON A TRADEMARK

Wear something slightly quirky. A bright scarf, or jacket, a slick of red lipstick. Cultivating your own style and taking care not to stick with corporate normcore will ensure you linger in people's minds, particularly in a room of suits.

MAKE A PLAN

Rather than just bidding a vague goodbye at the end of a conversation, say something specific, along the lines of: 'I'll email you later this week to arrange a meeting,' or 'I'll email you my CV tomorrow.' That way, you make a mental note to follow-up on the contact, and they'll be expecting your email.

FOLLOW UP QUICKLY

To ensure you don't slip out of your new contact's mind, make sure you get in touch quickly, and try to follow up with a question or an invitation, something it's easy and quick for them to respond to.

TIPS FOR THE FIRST-TIME NETWORKER

a. Go with someone you know, if possible with someone who's used to networking and who can introduce you.

b. Join a group and just listen – at some point you'll have something to say and you'll introduce yourself then OR someone will ask you to introduce yourself.

c. Don't drink too much! It's always better to stick to soft drinks if you can resist the lure of free wine.

d. Don't forget your business cards, and be liberal with them. You never know where opportunity could be hiding.

e. At the end of the night, write on the business cards you got what's the goal for the relationship and 'fun/personal facts' to help you remember the conversations you had with individual people.

f. Connect with anyone who gave you a card on LinkedIn.

SUCCESS IS CATCHING

You've probably heard about the theory of behavioural or social contagion. The term was first coined by French polymath Gustave Le Bon in the 19th century and it has since become the focus of extensive exploration by sociologists, psychologists and anthropologists. It describes the phenomenon of the spread of ideas and behaviours. It's proof of the fact that the people we surround ourselves with, whether socially or in our careers, 'rub off on us'.

Studies show that we are highly influenced by those closest to us. This applies in terms of health, financial well-being and emotion. If our close friends are overweight, we are more likely to be overweight. If our partner dies, we, too, are at a higher risk of death as a result. If we see other people around us giving money to charitable causes, we are more likely to do the same thing ourselves. These are obvious examples. But there are plenty more subtle ones.

In his TED talk 'The Hidden Influence of Social Networks', social psychologist Nicholas Christakis examines the impact of social contagion on a range of phenomena, from obesity to mental health. He maps connections between these that relate to 'clusters' of networks, and posits the question: Is contagion a consequence of induction, homopholy or confounding? I'm going to explain what he means by this below, unpacking how each of these explanations might apply to the advancement of women in the workplace:

A) Induction

In short: one person does something and others copy; more follow, and so on. Gender-conscious networks and female leadership have a positive influence on more junior women in the workplace. We witness women rising through ranks and feel empowered, confident and ambitious, striving for the same advances ourselves.

B) Homopholy

In short: we like people who are like us. This is a strong business case for corporations to buy into agendas around diversity and equality in the workplace. Strong women want to work for organizations who see them as a priority. Visible networks and programmes that support equality in the workplace are indicators of a work community that chimes with women's own values. Such workplaces make far more tempting long-term prospects for new female recruits than those that seem fustier and more tokenistic.

C) Confounding

In short: environmental exposure causes a similar reaction in a group of people. For example, two women in a department both perform better due to a new leadership programme. Using the same tools, both are able to advance more quickly than they would have done without the intervention.

Christakis concludes that the answer is a combination of the three. I believe the same is true of women's advancement. We need strong female leaders to spark induction; we need a critical mass of women to create a climate where homopholy is possible, and we need organizational interventions that inspire women to put themselves forward.

Everyone, men and women alike, benefits from a workplace where diversity of perspective is nurtured and where there is a healthy gender balance running right the way through an organization. There is plenty of research to tell us this. Now we need to get on with changing our workplaces to facilitate greater equality, so women who have the potential to lead can realize this. Let's work towards a future where talent and capability are the biggest predictors of career success. Exceptional women should be just as likely to outshine as exceptional men.

THE BEST WOMEN'S NETWORKS

If you aren't sure where to start, check out our list (below) of some of the best women's networking organizations in Europe, the UK and the US.

WORLDWIDE

Lean In
Set up by Facebook COO Sheryl Sandberg after her book of the same name sparked a movement. There are now Lean In circles in 150 countries worldwide.
www.leanin.org

Women In Technology International
US based organization with outposts all over the world.
www.witi.com

Women's Forum
An global organisation that aims to bring together global business leaders to strengthen the influence of women throughout the world.
www.womens-forum.com/news/womens-forum-global-network

PWN Global
A global business network striving for gender-balanced leadership. Facilitates the connection of women in leadership roles and supports shared knowledge and experience in businesses seeking greater diversity.
www.pwnglobal.net

Girls In Tech
With chapters all over the world, Girls In Tech is a global non-profit with the aim of supporting women entering the industry and building start-ups.
www.girlsintech.org

Double You
A community of 'business-minded women', supporting networking and inspiration through their retreats around the world.
www.doubleyou.life

UK

Women In Business Network
A networking organization with franchised groups around the UK for women who want to network. Many run their own businesses.
www.wibn.co.uk

Bright Network
For students entering the workforce.
www.brightnetwork.co.uk

City Women
For senior professional women in London.
www.citywomen.org

US

National Association for Women Executives
Provides networking, advocacy and education for women working within businesses or running their own. It is one of the largest women's organizations in the US.
www.nafe.com

Elevate Network
A US-based network connecting women to other women in leadership positions to help support greater diversity and gender equality.
www.ellevatenetwork.com

EUROPE

Girlz In Web
France-based organization dedicated to the advancement and empowerment of women in tech.
www.girlzinweb.com

Geekettes
Based in Berlin, and with hubs everywhere from New York to Gaza, this organisation is dedicated to supporting female tech innovators.
www.geekettes.io

StartHer
A French organisation dedicated to supporting women working in tech.
www.starther.org

Pionniers Paris
A Paris-based organisation that supports tech start-ups with at least one woman on the leadership team
www.pionnieres.paris

ACKNOWLEDGEMENTS

It's said that everyone has at least one book in them. The problem is, most of us need a catalyst to help get it out. For me, that catalyst was the wonderful Delphine Poucet.

Thank you, Delphine, for our 'accidental encounter' on the flight from Frankfurt and for your support and encouragement – without you the book would never have seen the light of day.

To my amazing network of cousins and siblings who have always encouraged me across oceans – I would like to thank Hussein Hirji, Rahim Hirji, Rudy Karsan, Shelina Jessa and Salima Musaji in particular for their thoughts and ideas that helped find the necessary grit to see this through. To Zoe McDonald, George Edgeller, and John Bond – my editors and copy editors – thank you for your patience, counsel and honesty as we went through my first experience writing a book – I know it was challenging, so thank you for hanging in there!

To my co-authors Georgina and Marine – Thank you for sharing your amazing experiences, networks and for pushing this through in record time. It simply goes to show you how powerful our communities can be. Thank you, Hannah, for your incredible passion and dedication to Carbon Leadership. To my incredible mentors, thank you all for your advice – in particular I would like to thank Angela Pisano, Laurence Haziot, Alain Benichou, Tony Devore, Michele Stern, Johnna Torsone, and Jason Dies – all of you have shaped my views of leadership by being stellar examples yourselves. I have been very fortunate to have had the opportunity to work with all of you!

To my incredible son Qaahir, my quiet leader who taught me how to listen to everyone prior to talking, so that no one feels excluded. Thank you for listening.

To my amazing daughter Aliya, if everyone had a daughter like you, we could all achieve our dreams. Thank you for your constant encouragement ;-)

And finally, to my wonderful husband, Fayyaz: Thank you for pushing and challenging me. (I said it in black and white!) Your faith and wisdom has made me a better version of myself.

Shemin

I'd like to thank my family and especially my parents, Rosaine and Ludovic, and my brother, Thibaud, for being so supportive. No matter what new adventure I want to dive into, you're always there, pushing me forward, helping me to trust in myself... You have always known how to deal with my strong, sometimes stubborn, nature. I'd also like to thank my oldest friend, Pierrick, for sticking with me through tears and laughter. Also to Caroline. Both of you know how to be frank with me and shake me up so I keep on going despite my doubts.

I'd like to thank my dearest association, Girlz In Web, which enabled me to flourish as a feminist (and grow my career at the same time). Also, I'd like to thank the Sandbox network which helped me uncover my true self.

Finally, I'd like to thank my co-founders. I'll always remember the day I met Shemin to have coffee (and thank you Jason for that). Within an hour, we decided to launch Carbon Leadership. This common vision of empowerment created a strong bond. You helped advise me on one of the toughest decisions of my career, your enlightened vision and wisdom are invaluable to me. I'm proud to be your mentee, your partner. And thank you, Georgina. Our discussions have enabled me to get a fresh insight on what it is to be a strong, bright woman at the beginning of her promising career, tackling fearlessly the many obstacles that come her way.

Marine

Firstly, to my beautiful, courageous and resilient sister, Hannah Hill, who will be my best friend until the end of time. Thank you for your fierce loyalty, compassion and humour. Please continue to have faith in yourself, you're stronger than you know. To Mum, there are no words. Thank you for teaching me love and kindness. Everything I need to know about how to be a confident, smart, determined woman has always been right in front of me. Your faith in me has never wavered, and I share every success with you. Matt and Dan, thank you for forcing me to keep my wit and tongue sharp. I love you enormously. My wonderful co-authors, I am infinitely indebted to you for your priceless wisdom in these early years of my career. What a world we would live in if every young woman had mentors like you to lift her up. I am certain that you both will continue to inspire me throughout my life and our journey together. Finally, to Thomas West, without whose patience and support there may have been many steps untaken. Thank you for challenging me to know myself, and for keeping me laughing.

Georgina

AUTHOR BIOGRAPHIES

Shemin Nurmohamed is currently Country CEO for Pitney Bowes France. Prior to this role she held several CFO, Director and VP roles at local, EMEA and Global levels at several Fortune 500 companies. She has led several transformations concentrating on the motivation of emerging teams; developing innovative strategies; building leadership capabilities; enabling diversity and continuously encouraging entrepreneurial spirit in large multinational corporations.

Mrs Nurmohamed holds a BA in Chemistry from Cornell, an MA from the University of Toronto, and an MBA from Henley. She lives in Paris with her husband and two children.

Marine Aubin is a French consultant and entrepreneur, expert in innovation management and digital strategy. She is a passionate feminist, involved in several organizations that work to empower and support women in the workplace and society.

Georgina Hill is a British national currently completing a BA degree at Newcastle University. Georgina began her career as a marketing manager at a French technology startup in Paris, where she met her future Carbon Leadership co-founders. Passionate about socio-economic justice for women and minorities, Georgina brings a fresh and international perspective to female leadership.